BRAVEMOUTH

BRAVEMOUTH

LIVING WITH BILLY CONNOLLY

Pamela Stephenson

ISIS

LARGE PRINT

Oxford

Copyright © Pamela Stephenson, 2003

First published in Great Britain 2003
by Headline Book Publishing Ltd.

Published in Large Print 2004 by ISIS Publishing Ltd,
7 Centremead, Osney Mead, Oxford OX2 0ES
by arrangement with
Headline Book Publishing Ltd.

British Library Cataloguing in Publication Data
Stephenson, Pamela
    Bravemouth: a year in the life of Billy Connolly. –
Large print ed.
    1. Stephenson, Pamela – Family
    2. Connolly, Billy, 1942–
    3. Entertainers – Scotland – Biography
    4. Comedians – Scotland – Biography
    5. Celebrities – Great Britain – Biography
    6. Large type books
    I. Title
    791'.092 [F]

ISBN 0–7531–9936–X (hb)
ISBN 0–7531–9937–8 (pb)

Printed and bound by Antony Rowe, Chippenham

To Adam, and all who have found solace in orange anoraks, fat-coated ladies, drunken walks and incontinence pants. To their creator and captivating nomads everywhere, and to those who wait for their return.

The author and publisher are grateful to the following for permission to use their copyright material:

"You're breaking my Heart" words and music by Harry Nilsson © 1972, EMI Blackwood Music Inc, USA. Reproduced by kind permission of EMI Songs Ltd, London WC2H 0QY. "It Had to be You" © Bantam Music Publishing Co. "Those lazy, hazy, crazy days of summer" © 1962 Edition Primus Rolf Budde KG, Berlin. "Kids" is reproduced by kind permission of EMI Music Publishing Ltd and BMG Music Publishing Ltd. "Near You" is reproduced by kind permission of Billy Connolly and Logo Songs Ltd.

For the most banal . . . to become an adventure, you must begin . . . to recount it . . . a man is always a teller of tales, he lives surrounded by his stories and the stories of others, he sees everything that happens to him through them; and he tries to live his own life as if he were telling a story.

But you have to choose: live or tell.

Jean-Paul Sartre, *Nausea*

CONTENTS

ACKNOWLEDGEMENTS

Once again I am enormously grateful to Val Hudson for her immense patience, support, sensitivity, good taste and expert guidance. Jo Roberts-Miller too deserves my gratitude for her excellent and tireless work, as does everyone at Hodder Headline who helped on this book. I am beholden to Steve Brown and Neha Bailhache for their insightfulness, and for the numerous ways in which each has supported me and our family. I also feel most grateful to Steve Martin for his encouraging critique, and to Dr Beverly Whipple for casting a professional eye over the manuscript. I would like to thank our staff through whose help I found time to write, especially Jock Edwards whose dedicated efforts were invaluable throughout the process, but also Andrew Tierney, Martine Hicks and Paul Hicks (who kindly took some of the family photos). I very much appreciate being allowed to quote and depict the people of my husband's sixtieth year, and am grateful to everyone whose name appears within these pages, especially my beloved subject, our children James, Cara, Daisy, Amy and Scarlett, and our grandson Walter. I would particularly like to thank Lynda Mosling as well as the anonymous people from whose letters I quoted in the Introduction. As that section reveals, I feel honoured to be trusted with your stories and, indeed, with those of everyone who wrote to me after the publication of *Billy*. I also thank you on behalf of my husband for your precious words. Bless you all in your search for courage, strength, healing and peace.

Introduction And Raison D'Être

I hated finishing *Billy*. The writing of it had allowed me to maintain an unexpected connection with my world-bestriding husband, for which I was most grateful. Due to the demands of his work, Billy was absent from home over much of that year in which I wrote his biography. As he sashayed through the Australian outback, spewed riotous curmudgeonry from a New York stage, sweet-talked the lens of a camera in Queenstown, and caught fine brown trout in icy Scottish streams, I travelled his life on a laptop from a Californian couch. For me it was a tender, uniting journey; for in tracing his trip from cradle-drawer to "incontinence knickers", he seemed as close as tears.

So I make no apologies for continuing, for myself at least (I would not presume for others), the delight of holding him consistently in my thoughts for the weaving of this new tapestry of his 2002 Earth Odyssey. This time I documented his sixtieth year, twelve months in which my husband was no less nomadic than he was the previous year. What follows is therefore a month-by-month almanac of an Internet-shy Ulysses by his Pentium Four Penelope.

My husband is an alpha-enigma: a man blessed with comedic peerlessness, literary panache, musical gifted-ness and acting brilliance who remains a warm, loving and delightful human being. I both love and admire him enormously, yet I have no intention of painting an idyllic picture of life with the Scottish beastie; for on a day-to-day basis, he can honestly annoy the crap out of me. At best, Billy's grasp of the realities of daily life is tangential. He cares deeply about the big stuff, but when it comes to picking up the dry-cleaning he can be as recalcitrant as a kipper in a kayak.

"Fuck, Pamsy," he's apt to spout while fleeing, "when I feel the urge to be useful, you'll be the first to know."

Billy is tough. Forsaken by his mother, rough-housed by relatives and violated by his father, he reached his nadir 'mid a saturnalia of "wee bevvies" and lived to tell the tale . . . or rather, to allow me to do so. Thankfully, Billy has grown happier since the imparting of his pain. As we drew close to the publishing of *Billy* he became most afraid of the pity of strangers. But the readers of *Billy* have been generous enough to let him know, in a variety of ways, that they appreciate him all the more for his ability to survive. For that, they'll go straight to heaven, since our hero has secretly needed nothing so much as that. Moreover, the hundreds of letters that came our way have proved to him that he's not alone. *I've never been able to tell anyone this before,* they often began, *but you've given me courage to do so . . .*

Heartwrenching revelations followed: of suffering, neglect, exploitation and despair.

I saw so much of myself in those pages was the tale of those who had similar learning difficulties to Billy, with many of the same attendant frustrations and school failures. *I especially relate to not being able to tell the time and tie shoelaces*, wrote one. For many, Billy's revelations led to the surfacing of memories and insights that had lain dormant for years: *It hit a chord so deep down inside me*, wrote one woman, *that once I had finished reading I started to cry uncontrollably . . . my own abuse was sexual from the age of five.* Another wrote, *Mental torture was the order of the day in my family too.*

There were so many who had buried shameful memories beneath layers of drinking, over-eating or other forms of self-destruction: *In between peeing my pants with laughter and sobbing from somewhere I'd been trying to forget, I was fighting this rising realisation that the words leaping off the page meant a lot more to me and my life than I was prepared to admit.* There are many ways to anaesthetise hurt: *I found comfort in a Mars Bar wrapper*, said one, and *I still sleep with a vegetable knife under my pillow*, confessed another. Others have yet to come to terms with their pain. The wife of an abused man wrote to me: *You are fortunate to know the full story of Billy's background. I am still waiting for his tears to come.*

As Billy and I read these letters, I could see in him a mixture of anguish and relief, and every now and again a glimmer of humour.

"Listen to this!" he cried. "*In a strange way it seems nice that it happened to someone as famous and gifted as Billy.*"

"Do you understand," I ventured as we sat cuddling on the sofa surrounded by pages of raw pain and beleaguered longing, "how much you have helped these people by telling them about you?"

"Poor bastards!" cried Billy. "I wish I could get my hands on the pricks who did this to them."

We both feel utterly grateful and honoured to have been trusted with these missives. They moved us most deeply, yet gave us cause to hope; for healing begins with the telling of sad, dark truths.

Even prior to his revelations, Billy, who certainly does not think of himself as a healer, had helped more people through the power of his comedy than I could ever reach in a lifetime of providing psychotherapy. Lynda Mosling, the mother of a once-fit, strapping and bearded nineteen-year-old who died from leukaemia at twenty, wrote:

Dear Billy

You may wonder why I am writing a thank you letter to you — given that you didn't know of Adam's existence, let alone his death. But I have learned to say the things that mattered to him — and you mattered to him . . . he spent hours in hospital listening to your audio and video tapes that rendered him helpless with laughter.

Adam always loved eccentric people, hated pretentiousness of any kind and would seek out real and honest people to share his sense of humour with. During leave from hospital he was able to come and see you live — a delight he held on to in his final days.

You were everything he enjoyed and respected in a person and insisted on several quotes of yours being included in his funeral. So I thank you for the pleasure you gave him throughout his short life and the pleasure you continue to give my husband and I, who laugh when remembering Adam's response to you when we continue to watch your videos.

He was our only child and we miss him dreadfully, but thanks to you we can remember him doubled up with laughter, even in the days he was dying.

Take care — life would be worse without you.

There have been many such thank-you letters over the years. It would not come as any surprise to those who wrote them that researchers at Glasgow Caledonian University have established scientifically that listening to Billy's comedy can substantially increase people's tolerance to pain. In the aftermath of *Billy*, my husband's success has finally been understood for what it truly is: triumph over his abusers, and a metaphor for others' hope.

Now, as "windswept and interesting showbiz personality", raucous raconteur and savage gypsy lover, Billy's revenge has been good living; and there was plenty of that in his sixtieth year. Billy has never been shy about either his wealth or his appearance.

"I'm not the best looking guy in the world," he's apt to tell his audiences.

"Aaahhh . . ." they chorus, in uniform sympathy.

"Oh, don't feel sorry for me," he smiles disarmingly. "I'm loaded."

But for Billy, all rewards are transient. At some level he still expects to be "found out", as he puts it, to be tapped on the shoulder by a man with a stop watch. "That's it." The man will be stern and uncompromising. "Time's up. No more swanning round the world for you. It's back to being plain William Connolly: welder, dry-cleaning-picker-upper, and joiner of queues."

Even now, after nearly forty years in the limelight, Billy still has a curious relationship with his fame. This is not unusual for a person who has come to public attention, for celebrity is invariably disruptive for the psyche.

"Keith Richards knows me!" Billy will say proudly, like a freezing autograph-hunter lingering outside Langan's Brasserie. Though essentially more comfortable in his skin than ever before, the injured little boy in Billy still harbours a niggling doubt that he deserves the luck, success and fame he holds, or that he should be celebrated, even by means of a party for his forthcoming sixtieth birthday (you will see how hard it was to pull that off). Turning sixty, however, must be a surprise for anyone.

"I hope I die first," he says touchingly.

"Don't be selfish," I retort.

CHAPTER
ONE

It's My Fucking Head!

Billy Connolly, twenty-two-year-old reluctant welder, tattered troubadour and "See-you-Jimmy" jokester, sauntered cheerfully down Renfrew Street looking for a pint. In his bull's-blood velvet trousers, brown leather reindeer boots with curled-up pointed toes, black-and-white-striped Tunisian duffel coat and haywire hairdo, he was quite a sight for the generally conservative folks he passed outside Woolworth's, the dance hall and the bagpipe-maker's shop. For them, his shagginess was the worst offence.

"Wha?" demanded one out loud. "Did ye glue yer heid and dive in a barber's midden?"

"There's many a man broke his nose with his mouth," threatened Billy, sending him scuttling backwards into an alleyway. An engineer from Stephen's Shipyard came careering out of the bus terminal with a half-eaten fish supper stuffed in his pocket.

"Eh, how's it goin', Ho Chi Minh!"

That was the nickname he had acquired in the shipyards after sprouting eight inches of straggly, reddish-brown goatee. Billy nodded reservedly and strode on. At that time, long whiskers were so rare in Glasgow he was quite used to the attention. Strangers called him Sammy Baird, after a footballer who played for Rangers FC, and even children would sing out a rhyme as he strolled by:

> *Greasy baird,*
> *Tuppence a yaird!*

A couple of buses were idling outside the Pavilion Theatre, a building of yellow Cotswold stone that was a favourite destination for parties of women from rural institutes or working groups, all champing to see popular variety acts. Billy, on the other hand, had just enjoyed a very different kind of theatrical experience: a rehearsal of one of the electrifying rock bands that made their way to Glasgow during the sixties. He loved to slide into an upper circle back seat at the Apollo and view these gods of exotica strutting their stuff. Deep Purple, Medicine Head, Fleetwood Mac, Status Quo and Black Sabbath: he eventually witnessed every single one, courtesy of his similarly hairy pals in the backstage crew. Billy's own stage career at that point was limited to sporadic gigs with the Skillet Lickers, an informal group of folkies he'd convened to play small, rowdy pubs and badly lit halls.

A squat, slightly tipsy woman, with chubby woollen coat and waved hair, stepped off the bus right in front of him.

"Och Mother Mary," she said, catching sight of Billy. "Look at this!" She tucked her box of liqueur chocolates under her arm and teetered closer for a better look.

"Look at the baird!" she cried, reaching for his bewhiskered face. "Can I give it a wee tug for luck?"

"Certainly," sighed Billy. He obligingly stuck out his chin and bent down to her height. Taking it in her rough little hand, she rang it like a dinner bell.

"Oh, that's lovely!" She smelled of whisky and new perm.

Billy expected her to let go within a reasonable time frame, but she had other ideas.

"Bettyeeeeeeeeee!" she called to her friend. Still firmly clutching his beard, she took off smartly round the corner with Billy in tow. There was no escape from this pugnacious little terrier. Bent over like a half-open penknife, he pulled and protested in vain. Those petite, working-class women might look like they're made of marshmallows, but they're as strong and fight-smart as Glasgow's hard men and can redesign your head as soon as look at you. When they found Betty, she was clutching her handbag between her knees so she could finish a packet of shortbread.

"Look what I've found!" Billy was dragged closer like a big stupid dog. "You want a wee tug for luck?"

"Aye, Sammy Baird," said Betty with her mouth full. She shoved the biscuits into her bag and wiped her crumby hands on the tail of Billy's beard before giving it several good, firm yanks.

"Oh, Missus, give me a break," yowled Billy. "Nobody needs that much luck."

★ ★ ★

Almost forty years later, on the very first day of the year, that lucky beard had become bright purple. Its owner was peering at himself in a magnifying mirror, eyeglasses balanced on the end of his nose, deftly reapplying "Purple Haze" punk hair colour with a dilapidated toothbrush. He wore an exaggerated sneering expression that caused his moustache to splay out at a convenient elevation away from his upper lip. Billy's initial colour choice had been apple green, which had gone down a storm at a Celtic football match the previous summer. Celtic Football Club functions not only as my husband's team, but also as the focus of his unparalleled primal passion, all-consuming religion and vanishing excuse. The players' green and white hooped jerseys are visual homing devices that lead him to sit freezing and anxious in similarly coloured clothing for ninety minutes at a time, with fist, roar, sigh and yowl at the ready. That season, Billy just went one step further and added team spirit to his beard.

For Billy, facial hair has vast potential to elicit meaning from the universe.

"A primary-coloured beard is a perfect arsehole-detector," he says, referring to the tendency of dreary folk (or "beige people" as he would call them) to reveal themselves in the presence of someone whose unusual appearance upsets them. Other useful pursed-lips spotting aids have included his "Lesbians Unite" T-shirt, his "Mexican Day of the Dead" cowboy boots (black with red skulls, silver scythes and blue skeletons), and his favourite pair of dangly gold earrings.

Billy's first attempt at turning "aubergine", as he prefers to call it, proved acutely agonising. "Before applying colour, you must first bleach it white," he explained, providing a beauty crisis post-mortem with all the authority of a junior colourist from an Inverness hair salon. Billy had mixed the wrong strength of peroxide with his "delicate facial bleaching powder", resulting in the loss of several layers of chin-skin. This particular afternoon he was thankful for his steady hand, especially since it was the day after Hogmanay, or New Year's Eve. He noted with satisfaction that, as a teetotaller of eighteen years or so, he was probably one of the very few people in Scotland who was not bemoaning the presence of a thumping sore head.

Once satisfied that each bristle was thoroughly coated, Billy glanced at his watch. Three minutes past four. Excellent! He'd wash this lot off in just twenty minutes then join the family in time for afternoon tea. He breathed a sigh of contentment. All his children had gathered at Candacraig, our Highland retreat, for the winter break. He could hear his first grandson, nine-month-old Walter Valentine, squealing delightedly above a cacophony of general merriment. Walter had the ability to turn Billy's scowl into a doting beam at any time, and the family was well aware of it. For example, if Walter was part of the equation, his early-morning grumpiness could easily be assuaged. That very morning, Billy's thirty-three-year-old son James had amused the rest of the family with two contrasting impressions of his father's imminent arrival at breakfast:

One (without Walter's presence):

"Fucking growl grumble fuck grumble waking me for fucking breakfast growl grumble fuck bloody fuck middle of the damn night . . ."

Two (with Walter sitting there in his highchair surrounded by Weetabix goo):

"Hellooo my little man! How's my wee darlin' this morning?"

In fact, Walter had become the family's dangled carrot for whatever form of manipulation it had in mind for its figurehead. His teenage daughters have perfected the trick, as in:

"Hey, Dad, how about we take Walter to Gap and buy me a new pair of jeans?"

Billy took a face flannel and held it under the warm tap. He rubbed his goatee vigorously until the flannel was itself a vivid mauve, then rinsed and rinsed until his bristles zinged with their fine new depth of hue. He stood back to admire them in the longer mirror, gave them a final brush with a small boar-bristle instrument he kept just for that purpose, then leapt downstairs and strode cheerfully into the living room.

His family was in mid mind-wrestle, engaged in a trivia game called Who's in the Bag? It was the turn of his youngest daughter, thirteen-year-old Scarlett, to give the clues so her team mates could guess the names of famous personalities. She was draped upside-down on a round ottoman, her long ballerina limbs practising entrechats in the air.

". . . singer and she's . . . I think she's French . . . sings ballads . . . thin, beats her chest a lot . . ."

12

"Celine Dion," her team chorused, "and she's Canadian!"

It was Amy's turn. At fifteen, her approach was a little more languid. She twisted her honey-blonde hair into a wavy ponytail. "Plays Monica in *Friends* . . ."

"Too easy!" complained Daisy, who had celebrated her eighteenth birthday the day before. She was balanced on all fours, giving Walter a horsy-ride. His parents, James's younger sister Cara and her boyfriend Jonnie, watched warily from the fireside rug.

Scarlett picked up another card. The pressure was on.

"Oh! oh! oh! . . . um . . . DAD!"

"Billy Connolly!" cried his other children.

"Right."

Billy stood paralysed behind the group, as if he'd just entered a parallel universe.

"Was that really in the game?" he asked incredulously. "Was I really a clue?"

"Dad," said James, barely even glancing round, "your hands are purple."

Five days later, just after we'd returned to our Los Angeles home, Billy Connolly, board-game clue, beige-abater and punk-whiskered grandpa, took his startling new look to meet a film director on the back lot of Universal Studios, California. They were to discuss his possible appearance in a movie called *Timeline*, adapted from the Michael Crichton sci-fi novel, to play a role that was unlikely to have been intended for a man with a purple beard. On a

13

moisture-less afternoon the retinue of stunt men, make-up artists and film technicians bustling between sound stages, make-up trailers and craft services glanced quizzically at the passing shabby-chic Scot with the grapey goatee. Billy has finally achieved the quest of a lifetime: to turn dishevelment into an art form. From the neck down, in his car-crushed linen slacks and "Voyage" T-shirt, he was all south of France swish and crumpled intensity. The director he met was affable and business-focused, tactfully reserving the most essential artistic question until the very last moment of their "meet and greet".

"And would you be willing to change the colour of your facial hair?" he enquired with uncharacteristic timidity.

"It's my head." Billy shrugged agreeably. "I can do whatever the fuck I want with it."

It is not the kind of riposte that is usually heard in Hollywood, but then Billy has become known there for being brave of mouth, inspiring our neighbour Eric Idle to dub him "Brave-mouth". Indeed, it is unlikely to have escaped your notice that he tends to employ speech, topics and style of delivery that defy the boundaries of what is normally considered acceptable in polite company. That is, of course, a precious element of his comedy, for he treads where others fear to go and is all the funnier for it. But he is also far from cowardly in environments that are not bastions of free expression, such as elevators, doctors' waiting rooms and high school meetings. As a matter of fact, the more conservative Billy's surroundings, the more he's inclined to go for it.

Billy is not just brave of mouth. He is also brave of almost every part of his body, especially feet (black-polished toenails), nipples (pierced) and ears (lobe jewellery in both). Billy's head-hair has changed over the years from skunk-streak to bouffant bovver-boy, from eighties layers to matinee-idol. Style-wise, his beard has morphed from Che Guevara gaucho glamour to wrecked roadie rats' tails; from D'Artagnan dashingness to film star stubble. It has served him as pacifier (he strokes it when he's nervous), fashion accessory, and erstwhile weapon. "C'mere and let me give you a beardy!" he used to growl at his squealing children, when they were small enough to be swept into his arms and nuzzled with his prickly chops. Frankly, his moustache can cause injury. When kissing him I always have to remember to aim straight, or approach from above. If any upward adjustment needs to be made once lips are in close contact, I'll get sharp prickles up my nose. I think of it as the opposite of shark feeding. I learned in Bora-Bora that if you're ever hand-feeding a deep-sea predator you must remember to bring your arm upwards to its mouth or you'll likely lose it. The formula is easy: Shark up, Billy down.

I am not usually given to wondering why in particular Billy changes any aspect of his appearance, for he has a very original sensibility when it comes to clothing and body-decoration, and has loved to confront people with an outrageous new look since he was in his early twenties. At the beginning of the year, however, I thought I detected a subtle surge in the level of urgency with which he approached this change of hue. At first I wondered if his new, unmistakable purpleness was spawned by his fury that he had recently been mistaken for another well-known British man.

"You're him, aren't you?" A man in stone-washed jeans and an eighties haircut had sidled up to Billy at a country music fair. "Would you mind giving me your autograph? I've got all your records."

"Sure . . ." said Billy suspiciously, "but who do you think I am?"

"Oh come on!" replied the man, taking out a grubby video of *Life of Brian*. "You're John Cleese!"

"I'm afraid I'm not," said Billy, quite affably.

"Ah!" winked the man. "Incognito, huh?"

"No." Billy was searching for an escape route. "I'm . . . er . . . I'm a Scottish comedian."

"Sure you are." The man winked conspiratorially. "Don't worry . . . I'll keep your secret!"

Billy has never confessed this to John himself, but his explosive, action-oriented reply lost the Monty Python star an ardent fan.

I am thankfully spared such problems, for I am no longer in show business and hardly resemble anyone who is. I began my stage career at five years old, as a dancing mammal in my ballet school's production of *The Teddy Bears' Picnic*. It was staged in a local hall, the centre of social events in the small Australian suburb of Sydney where I was raised, so everyone in town saw the pee leaking from my bear suit. I eventually recovered from that singular embarrassment, and went on to perform perfectly continent dancing solos in the roles of assorted fairies, flowers and the Spirit of Winter. In the process I discovered that performing afforded me a pleasure that I nurtured and enjoyed for another thirty years, until I segued into a different usage of my lifelong examination of human behaviour: the practice of psychology.

But my six-year-long training in the latter failed to help me immediately detect that Billy's pugnacious beard-colouring was linked to his desire to increase his "fuck-you" quotient in the light of his approaching sixtieth birthday. It seems so obvious, with hindsight. Of course he must have been having some wobbly feelings about turning sixty, but at the time I was a little slow to recognise it. Perhaps that was because Billy is not a person who ever cared to disguise his physical signs of aging. Youth-enhancing paraphernalia such as hair replacement, peels and plastic surgery are not his style, and he would never simply darken his bristles in an attempt to look younger, unless of course a movie role demanded it. To illustrate his distaste for such artificial youth-seeking behaviours, Billy is apt to perform a side-splitting visual joke where he sweeps his entire head of shaggy locks to one side and plasters them flat in what he calls an "honest I'm not bald" comb-over.

As a matter of fact, Billy is somewhat averse to hair cuts of all kinds, and absolutely loves his "Old Father Time" look when his beard and hair become ridiculously white and bushy. In truth, I have observed that Billy does the very opposite of most middle-aged people, by trying to look older than he actually is. He once took the children to the mall at Christmas and was thrilled to discover he looked more like Santa than Santa.

Since I met Billy in 1979, I have watched him enter each new decade of his adult life in idiosyncratic fashion. Upon the arrival of his forties he made a healthy, clean sweep of many elements in his life, including cigarette smoking, drinking and party drugs. In those days there was only slight awareness of the ticking of the clock. For example, on stage he began to wonder out loud whether Grecian 2000 would work on his pubes, and announced that his nasal hair was accelerating for reasons best known to itself. "I used to cut it once every thirty years, but now it's twice a month," he confided to audiences. "I'm presuming my body knows what it's doing, but I'm very baffled. I'm wondering what's going to happen to me that I'm going to need long nasal hair to deal with it."

Billy's fifth decade brought a move to the United States, a resurgence of his movie career, and two pierced nipples. Remembering the latter gave me pause, especially when, back in Los Angeles in the second week of January, I noticed a magazine for piercing aficionados sitting on the passenger seat of his car. It occurred to me he might be considering some type of exceptionally alarming body modification to serve as a unique age-defying mechanism. What would it be? I wondered. Had his joke about the man with holes in his willy prompted him to follow suit?

"Sixty. Fucking sixty." I heard him on the phone to a Scottish pal and gave myself a big fat "Duh!" *Of course* the thought of it was quite alarming for Billy, despite his protestations to the contrary. His own father was close to his death by then.

"Yeah, I think I'll get hair extensions for my sixtieth. Or maybe a blue rinse . . ."

There it was, as plain as the banjo tattoo on his fist. I finally realised that, though a whole eleven months away, his Sexagesimus nevertheless loomed portentously in his subconscious mind, not as the beginning of decrepitness but as The End of All Windswept-and-Interestingness and the advancement of beigeness. On top of that, his participation in *Timeline* was still uncertain. I watched him mope about the house and wondered, what would be his strategy for dealing with such an impasse? Perhaps he should follow a life-long remedy and escape to the seaside.

In mid-January, Billy took off for a brief sojourn in the Mexican coastal town of San José del Cabo, way down the Baja cape, near the Finisterra, or Land's End, where the Sea of Cortez meets the Pacific Ocean. San José is a delightful seventeenth-century town of warm-toned adobe Spanish colonial buildings, quaint village inns and contemporary townhouses. Its shady plazas branch out into both cobbled streets and modern boulevards, while sun-bleached archways lead to tiled inner courtyards with sprinkling fountains and palm-fringed benches. It's a far cry from its nearby sister town Cabo San Lucas, the spring break playground of American undergrads. They bar hop along its crowded resort strip from the Giggling Marlin to the Cabo Wabo Cantina till midnight, then bounce frenetically at El Squid Roe until four in the morning. Billy's preference is unquestionably the less touristy San José, where the pace is lazy and the townspeople talkative. He can sit by the ocean and play his banjo, keeping an eye out for the sudden appearance of shooting sea-spray. These herald a graceful arcing of the vast, V-shaped tails of California grey whales, migrating creatures who have swum nearly a thousand kilometres to frolic in the warm Baja sea.

Within three days of his arrival, Billy's punk puce goatee had become *cotilleo*, the Hispanic equivalent of the "talk of the steamie". In the early part of the last century in Glasgow, the steamies, or public laundries, were the founts of all gossip, but in San José it is the ever-crowded open-air market place that spawns rumours, rites and recriminations. Set in the town square opposite a huge Spanish colonial church, the Iglesia San José, the market is a smorgasbord of ceramics, raffia bags, silver jewellery, and cheesecloth blouses.

After three days of observing Billy swish round their village, the local people of San José became thoroughly intrigued by El Barba Morado (the purple-bearded one), as he had come to be known.

"Buenos días, Señor . . . Señora . . ." Billy took to bowing Spanish-style to anyone who made eye-contact during one of his afternoon strolls.

"Mr Connolly . . . it's yourself!" was often the disappointing reply. Even British tourists are known to straggle down to Baja for a bout of tacos, tequila and real estate roulette.

I've tried to understand my gringo husband's *affaire* with Mexican culture, but have yet to do so fully. Glaswegians rarely see the sun at home, as Billy says, and their bodies are naturally a whiter shade of blue unless they're given to visiting bronzing salons such as "TANeriffe" in the Byres Road. I doubt, though, that Billy's passion for things Hispanic is limited to the weather. I've seen glimpses of his curious identification with Ernest Hemingway, a fantasy in which he sees himself in an ivory linen suit with wooden cane, sipping iced tea beneath a ceiling fan in a bar in Old Havana.

On one particular mid-January afternoon, he sat in a wicker chair reading banjo magazines on his San José hotel veranda, ignoring the crocheted hammock strung artfully from wall to wall. Billy views the latter as a human snare.

"Hammocks are nature's way of telling you you're getting old," he mourns. He puts them in the same category as bean-bag chairs.

"Is there a jacaranda on your veranda?" I asked him on the phone, referring to a rhyming gag we invented. We both love the flowering Australian tree beneath whose violet canopy I picnicked as a child.

"No, but I'm not short of a cactus." Billy is unnaturally drawn to the spiky little succulents, for they come in the rudest shapes.

"What's the weather like?" I was to join him the following day for a long weekend.

"Brilliant," he said. "I'm as happy as a wee clam."

I pictured him swishing around in his sandals. I had been longing to have a brief escape myself. Quite apart from the demands of our three youngest daughters who still live at home, my private practice, research and teaching make me LA-bound for most of the year. On top of that, Billy's schedule of global touring means that it is not at all easy for him and me to be together.

"I'll see you tomorrow," I said. "One loves one." That is usually his line. We began our oft-repeated routine after we saw John Cleese and Connie Booth do a hilarious, 1920s ocean-liner deck scene for a charity event in London called *The Secret Policeman's Ball*.

"One loves one," Billy will say to me.

"One reciprocates," I will reply, "with ardour."

This is often followed by Billy's departure from the script:

"One would like to give one one."

I was excited to meet my smooth talker of a husband for a little alone-time. He was waiting for me after I exited customs, dressed in shorts and a shirt made from souvenir tea towels depicting scenic highlights of New Zealand. His legs were a little on the pinkish side.

"You need some Aloe Vera." I said.

"Hello, Vera!" he replied in a London accent.

We executed an obligatory, quick tour of San José, including the leafy Arroyo, once a refuge where eighteenth-century pirates could rest up between bouts of plundering, until the heat sent me wilting inside for a siesta. As usual, Billy had made many friends in this new town, people who worked in restaurants, sold books, or ran the local cigar store. They looked at me askance as though I were an interloper, putting a swift end to their hours of wild and wonderful *conversación* with the crazy Scottish gringo. I was sympathetic to their point of view, but now it was my turn.

"What do you think?" Back in our hotel room, Billy was admiring himself in a taupe, collarless shirt he'd picked up in the market.

"Hmm, situational aesthetic?" My friend Sharon introduced me to the term. It refers to the tendency of a tourist to convince himself he'd wear it back home. Usually a big mistake.

But Billy was so pleased with his find that on this occasion I back-tracked.

"No, it's really quite . . . ethnic." In fact it was almost beige, but the hand-stitched embroidery saved it. Billy will frequently buy such an item, wear it for a day, then let it sit at the back of his closet until the school jumble sale. In Los Angeles, some people actually have careers as closet organisers. They sweep into your life with chic, matching hangers, shoe-trees and plastic bags, and make pronouncements like "Let's get rid of everything that's not Dolce or Dries!" I considered hiring one of the bossiest "stylers" around, to "do" Billy's side of our shared closet, just for the enjoyment of seeing her face when confronted by his idio-syncratic collection of Jo Bananas, sixties memorabilia, Vivienne Westwood and cowboy unchic. Personally, I am reasonably tolerant of the fact that certain Californians are given to hiring all kinds of supposed quality-of-life enhancers, such as feng shui diviners or dog therapists, but for Billy they come under the heading of "What possesses them?"

We lazed away the rest of the day on his horsehair mattress and embroidered Mexican pillows, until the sun finally drooped and it was cool enough to venture out again. We made a bee-line for an outdoor cantina to scoff shrimp fajitas followed by peppercorn ice-cream, and wandered into the town square, the Plaza Mijares, where a horribly discordant musical line-up was providing the Saturday night entertainment for strolling townsfolk. Guitars, trumpets and synthesisers alternated between Mexican fiesta music, hymns and fifties American crooning. Two ancient speakers produced ear-wrenching squeaks, while the stone dance floor was commandeered by teenagers on bicycles, younger children playing "chicken", and a hobo solo-shuffling to "That's Why the Lady is a Tramp". The incongruity of the "Zorro" setting and a Frank Sinatra song is the kind of sight we both love to witness in foreign countries; like rap artists in Bali or Peruvian ballet dancers.

We slipped away to a side street, where a couple of Huichol tribespeople were selling handicrafts they'd made and transported all the way from their home in far-off Sierra Madre Occidental. They had wonderful masks, bowls and jewellery, all decorated with tiny, rainbow-coloured glass beads pressed into beeswax. There were "yarn pictures" too, bright, surreal creations that depicted visions the artists had experienced under the influence of peyote, a hallucinogenic drug derived from the mescal cactus. Billy was very taken with the work.

24

"That old mescaline has some effect," he said admiringly. I looked at him sideways.

"Don't even think about it." I so admire the way he managed to recover from two decades of substance abuse, but I know there are times when he misses it.

I left San José on an early morning flight. Billy half-opened his eyes as I kissed him goodbye.

"You were dreaming rather noisily," I said.

"Och . . ." Suddenly gaining consciousness, he smiled bemusedly. "Eh, aye, it was terrible! I murdered Paul McCartney and buried him in Glasgow. At the traffic lights!"

"You were yowling."

"Well, it was a terrible thing to do. Murder the most famous rock star in the world. Blame ice-cream and jetlag."

He sat up and glared at me suspiciously.

"Are you going to come up with some shrinky explanation?"

"No way," I replied. "Sometimes an ex-Beatle is just an ex-Beatle."

On January 26th, Australia Day, a week after I had returned to school runs, dental appointments and professional life, Billy travelled back to LA from Mexico with five beige embroidered shirts in his suitcase. For the journey he had chosen a pale-brown suede jacket, chinos and loafers. A British man wearing a navy blazer and white shoes spotted him in the elevator at LA International Airport.

"You're dressed nicely!" he remarked unkindly.

He couldn't have picked a worse time. Billy really took it to heart.

"I've gone off these clothes," he sighed when he got home, moping over a cup of tea.

"You look very handsome," I soothed him. "Don't let that rude person influence you."

"I can't help it. The pants are kind of beige . . ."

"Nah, they're stone," I insisted.

"Chill, Dad, you're cool," yawned the girls.

Billy's obsession with avoiding beige has not abated one iota, in fact it's getting worse, and is now so well-known that even people he doesn't know send him newspaper clippings containing "beige updates", like the newspaper clipping Pam Alden sent him from Australia:

*Stephen and Rachael are proud to announce
the arrival of Beige Rochelle*

Billy cheered up when a few friends arrived for my annual Australia Day "Beauty and Terror" dinner party, which was far from beige. I grew up with vivid colours. The crimson warratah flower, the bright-gold wattle, stinky-pink hibiscus and the clear, sapphire skies; as a child I took them for granted until I began to travel and discovered that much of the world was muted-down.

I was born in New Zealand, a greeny-blue place to which I am drawn for its peacefulness, beauty and down-to-earthness. My childhood summer holidays were spent cavorting with my cousins on Takapuna Beach, just north of Auckland, climbing trees in the family orchard, and mucking about in boats on the glorious, still unspoiled inlets of the Bay of Islands. But I have been an Australian citizen from the age of four. Every twenty-sixth of January I am driven to decorate the house with Australiana kitsch: vinyl kangaroos, blue plastic sharks (that's where the *terror* comes in) and a five-foot platypus that takes an hour to inflate. At each place setting there was a tiny Australian flag as well as the black, red and yellow Aboriginal insignia, and furry kookaburras, wombats (Billy's favourite animal), possums and koalas.

James, who now lives in Los Angeles, was the first to turn up, wearing a Balinese shirt and silver ethnic jewellery. In contrast to his father, he has chosen to oppose the whole notion of hairiness by frequently sporting a modish, fully shaved head. He was handed a balloon-pump the minute he walked in the door.

"I love you, Pamsy," he said to me as he surveyed the decor, "but as a hostess you're seriously scary."

The candy of my childhood, Fedexed at the last minute by bemused Aussie pals, was bountifully displayed: Celtic-coloured Minties (chewy white parcels), flaming Jaffas (orange-shelled chocolate), Cherry Ripes (coconut, chocolate and cherry) and the deliciously crunchy, chocolate-covered honeycomb that Billy refers to as *Violent* rather than *Violet* Crumble Bars.

"It's like Toblerone," he complains, "yet another aggressive sweetie. Why do people insist on making chocolate bars that hurt you?"

We usually serve barbecued food, accompanied by such standards as Vegemite soup and Fairy Bread, which is a buttered slice dotted with multi-coloured "sprinkles". People think I'm mad when I bully them into standing for the Australian National Anthem and joining in a between-courses sing-song of such popular ditties as "Waltzing Matilda" and "Tie Me Kangaroo Down", but I don't care. If I play my cards right I can usually talk Billy into giving us a rendition of "Purple Haze" on his own didgeridoo. I know it all sounds cheesy, but I do miss the place.

Halfway through the Pavlova, I realised that Billy had disappeared. I found him alone outside on the porch tinkling on his banjo, the musical choice of the antisocial, as Eric Idle calls it. I approached him with caution. It can be dangerous to try to undermine Billy's focus on what is *truly* important to him, that is, what I call the three F's: Fishing, Football, and Frailing (banjo playing). Anyone who does, becomes an *agent provocateur*, at whom he is liable to feel quite justified shouting "Whattt?" for having the audacity to impinge on the private Tao of Billy. Now, as annoying as that can be for his cohabitants, there is a reason for this, and it is not just bloody-mindedness.

Right from childhood, Billy was thoroughly ornery. Can anyone really blame a child for unruly behaviour when his entire universe is dangerous, chaotic, unyielding and dark? Readers of *Billy* will know that, born in an impoverished wartime community, he was abandoned by his mother when he was only four. He was then raised by an abusive trio of father and two

28

aunts, and also suffered at the hands of sadistic brutes masquerading as school teachers. There was no physical escape for him, but Billy unconsciously created a safe haven within his own head; a horror-proof hidey-hole that no one else could find. It was a way to shut out people and events, and in childhood it was necessary for his survival.

As Billy became a man, however, his hidey-hole remained in situ. It was no longer vital, for he had long since become capable of physically protecting himself; however, such mechanisms have a way of lingering. He still needs his reverie and, in a way, his aggressive stance against those who attempt to coax him away from it is a fight-or-flight response to a symbolic attacker. I have learned to disarm him with tenderness.

"How are you doing?" I asked him with all the gentleness I could muster with a dozen guests inside the house.

"Och, great," he said.

"Are you enjoying the party?"

"Och, aye. I just felt like a wee rest."

"Help me to understand why you're sitting out here." In the course of my psychology training I learned that confrontational questions beginning with "why" are generally best avoided. At first he did not answer. "Do you feel you need to dodge the crowd?"

"Dodge?" He was surprised. "No. You know, Pamsy, the appeal of being alone is not the absence of others, it's the presence of me. My mind flits all the time, and I think that irritates people around me, but it doesn't irritate me. It makes me very happy. When I'm with

29

other people I can't find me. I become the spectre at the feast, but I'm not me."

He was so eloquent about his immediate need for solitude, I had to let him be. As we sat together for a moment under a silhouette of palm trees, gazing far off at the twinkling freeways of the San Fernando Valley, I realised that this evening there was a calmness about him I had not previously seen for the entire month. The break in Mexico had done him a power of good and, as if to illustrate the truism that good things happen to people who can keep their anxiety in check, Billy heard the following day that his movie part was confirmed. He happily set about phoning and bustling, planning his forthcoming months. This lovely new air of optimism, however, lasted until he opened his newspaper on the very last day of January:

NEWSFLASH! WASHINGTON
The colour of the universe is not turquoise,
as astronomers previously thought, but beige.

"Well that's it," said Billy. "I'm totally doomed. Fuckwits in blazers are taking over the world."

CHAPTER
TWO

Elvis And The
Frog-People

You always know it's a good, icy winter when your bag of minnows freezes in the milk bottles on the windowsill. Billy found his bagaminnies, as Glaswegians call them, in the early morning, their faces staring at the ice, all dead. February snow had been falling all night, the first time he'd seen snowflakes since Christmas. From his eight-year-old experience, this was going to be a good fall. Not just ice, but a decent, thick, useful blanket. He had monitored its progress through his tenement window since dinner time, from the first contact of pristine flake on grimy window to the satisfying crackle underfoot as he made his way down the tenement stairs in the darkness, through the close, and along to the dingy midden behind the dental surgery. It was a good thing he'd found his father's torch. The treasure he sought could be a long way down inside any one of these filthy rubbish bins, piled over by ashes, bottles and putrid waste.

Every young midgie raker, or midden-diver, knew that ashes were to be the most avoided, for they'd paint his clothes a tell-tale greyish-white. "Pheoughh!" Billy tucked the torch under his chin and attempted to hold his nose with one hand while he dug with the other, but that required Houdini-like skills and risked the loss of his light source. Lest nausea overcome him, Billy backed away swiftly to the entrance of the alley for a moment to breathe the least foul air he could find, then skeltered back to furious sifting until his lungs again reached bursting point.

There were seven bins, and only one would be the dentist's. Inside the first few he met rotting vegetables, a sure sign he was on the wrong track. The fourth being taller than the others he had to take a run at it and leap high to knock off its lid, a dangerous exercise, since the noise might wake sleeping tenement dwellers. Once scaled, he balanced on the bin like a seesaw, its icy lip cutting into his stomach while he mucked about inside.

Clink! There it was! Pay dirt! The sound and feel of discarded, double-ended test tubes. He grabbed one from its bed of newly pulled teeth and allowed himself to slither back down to the ground, trying not to shatter it on the way. He made a swift exit and examined his prize beneath a green-tinged street lamp. "Hurrah!" he thought, removing the bloodstained cotton wool from inside his super new peashooter. He reached into his pocket, retrieved a handful of barley he'd pilfered from the grocer and loaded it into one of the two open ends of the test tube. Putting the other end to his lips, he gave it a whirl. Brilliant! He froze for a moment at the noisy ping of barley-seed on surgery window, then stashed his weapon under his jacket and turned to the most important part of the operation.

Shuffling around in the darkness, he stretched his arm behind each rubbish bin until he found where people had stacked the scraps of thin sheet metal they used as fireguards. He had to be careful, for it was so fine it could cut him like a knife. He gingerly grabbed the largest sheet he could find and wrenched it clunking and clattering out of its slot, while a satisfied glow warmed his frozen body.

What a coup this was! After school today, he and his friends would assemble their assortment of wooden egg-boxes, trays, cardboard strips, or a shovel from the coal bunker. They would haul them up to Bumbee, their name for an abandoned bomb site where damaged houses had never been rebuilt. The course had been marked in his mind since last snowfall, and now, finally, Billy was ready for the thrilling, treacherous race. He would take off at the top, come flying down the hill and across the path, then try to bail out at the fence before the prefab. All this, while shooting his opponents in the eye with his new barley-cannon. Billy set to work on the least jagged edge of his metal sheet, bending it towards him for a handle. Aye, it was a fine sled. Up there, on the Slopes of Bumbee, he would be King.

Once Billy outgrew the fireguard sheet, he entirely lost his passion for winter high jinks. Like most of his working-class friends, he never graduated to a pair of skis, and is as likely to head for the Scottish ski-centre of Aviemore as pick up a croquet stick. By the time he was a teenager, snow had become simply an irritant, preventing him from riding his bike, playing football, or adopting a sure-footed, casual swagger when girls were around, to emulate their idol Elvis Presley.

I have never managed to convince Billy that, in America, skiing is not a class-bound, exclusionary sport. Nor is it in New Zealand or Australia, although I didn't see snow until I was nearly twelve, and only learned to ski ten years ago when Billy and I relocated our family to California. In Los Angeles one can bask in hot sunshine in the morning, then drive for ninety minutes up into the San Bernardino mountains to ski at Big Bear in the afternoon. But on the first long weekend in February, Big Bear snow was thin on the ground, so the girls and I took off to Utah in search of nice, deep powder. Billy tagged along with his usual reluctance. "You look like the reserve crew of *Star Trek*," he said when we set off up the slopes the first morning, all kitted out with cushy, zippered goose-down suits, heated gloves and hi-tech boots. Billy decries the fact that such a simple experience as sliding has become so complicated, and utterly rejects the relative safety of modern snow sports equipment. As far as he's concerned, protective head gear and kneepads are for wimps and snow bunnies and I have to be quite stern to prevent him from undermining my stance about helmets for all. He trudged with us as far as the first ski-lift.

"You should come, Dad, you'd love it," pleaded Daisy, clipping on her snow-blades.

"What you really need," grumbled Billy, "is a shovel."

All those years ago, up on Bumbee, a shovel had afforded a boy the best chance for the ultimate thrill, for if he sat with the handle between his legs, he could hold on to it and steer. Then, if he spotted Tam Hughes the coal man from the lift-off point, he could time his take-off to meet him crossing the hill, and have a rare chance to slide under his horse.

"Yer mad! Away with you!" Tam would shout at the shovellers. They made his life a misery.

Instead of riding the chair-lift with us, up the heart-stopping face of Park City's Olympic downhill raceway, Billy did a U-turn and rode a shuttle bus into the local township. When one arrives at Salt Lake City airport, it is impossible to imagine from the flat, dry, surrounding plains that such a pretty winterland lies within an hour or two's drive. After leaving behind the ugliness of the endless Salt Lake suburbia, a land of peach-coloured mini-malls and concrete parking structures, the ascent into hills on narrower, fir-lined thoroughfares leads to a delightful world of snow-topped chalets and fairyland villages, set against a majestic backdrop of lofty peaks. Up here the malls are wooden toy-town buildings that smell of warm pine and cinnamon. Taking in the panorama from his bus seat, Billy was intrigued by the sight of an old silver mine that is part of the pioneering history of these once barely inhabited mountains. He was also charmed by the quaint town he found when he alighted from the bus, a cheery place of painted, wooden A-frame houses, all heavily laden down with snow. One had an iron bath hung on an outside wall that reminded him of a Scottish country bothy he knew near the gorgeous hills of Glenshee.

Billy tramped contentedly up and down the main street, hopping in and out of shops to peer at bargain-price wooden animal sculptures and silver-and-turquoise Navaho jewellery. He bought a heavy silver work bracelet, set with lumpy blue stones, then nipped jangling into a book shop and picked up a copy of *A History of God*. Billy has long been fascinated by the creation stories and deity conceptualisations by different cultures and religions at different times in their history. He sat in a coffee shop chewing over the God of Philosophers versus the God of Mystics until it was time to meet us in the skiers' cafeteria for soup and hot chocolate.

Back at the resort, he fought his way into the crowded food-station, past tables filled with ski-school toddlers, all fluffy sweaters and dinosaur hats. He stooped to retrieve one lonely, tiny yellow glove from a puddle on the floor, and laughed out loud at the size of it. Returning it to its tiny, giggling owner, he noticed that, rather than the string-connected woolly mittens his aunts had provided for him, these children wore padded, nylon beauties with zippers and clips to attach them to their pockets when not in use. He had to concede that the modern system was a clear improvement on the old.

One had to be quick to find a table in here. Billy scanned the room for one whose occupants were wrestling with their parkas and quickly claimed it. The first to arrive was Daisy, all pink-cheeked and puffed. The rest of us subsequently clonked ourselves into our seats with the customary grunts and sighs that accompany the removal of ski outerwear, and a litany of half-serious complaints about aching thighs, freezing noses and near-misses from stoned people on snow boards. Billy listened to all this indulgently, then sashayed off, full of broccoli and cheese, to enjoy one of his own favourite sports: watching people trying to stay upright on the uneven surface of the mid-mountain skating rink. I accompanied him for a while, eager to give my muscles a rest from their constant flexing, and because a wife does well, I think, to show an interest in her husband's pastimes. It is an unusual hobby, spotting perfectly nice people lose their footing, but Billy is hardly one for making things out of matchsticks.

"It would be rotten if someone really got hurt," he says, "but the shapes people make when they lose control just always make me roar."

He was rewarded for his journey as soon as he arrived, just in time to see a portly woman in a blue pompom hat swish helplessly into the air with both legs higher than her chest. She clutched wildly at a passing, interlocked couple, and all three of them came crashing down in a moving heap. Billy's chest began to heave, and a throaty chuckle emanated from his blue padded vest and tartan scarf. Beginning to giggle uncontrollably, he needed to sit down after the next sighting, when a stylishly outfitted man who was obviously proud and confident of his skating ability was hilariously up-ended by a small child in a green pixie hat who whooshed precariously in front of him. A tentative skater who had only just entered the rink and found the pace too fast tried to double back for safety, but in attempting a U-turn her legs took a series of fast-scraping jerks and she too ended up sprawled across the pathway of an oncoming group.

Billy's hysteria began to escalate beyond normal proportions. Although his enjoyment of the spectacle was clearly non-malicious, other onlookers began to look at him askance, and shifted sideways to be well beyond his flailing physiology. I had long since moved to higher ground and was trying not to giggle myself, for his laughter is very infectious. There were no seats by the rink, so he ended up sunk on his knees in snow-covered grass, and helpless with macabre mirth for close to half an hour. Every single lost foothold set him off again, being in essence a fine example of the quintessential slapstick comedy moment: slipping on a banana skin.

The following Tuesday evening, at the start of Billy's Los Angeles concerts at the Wilshire Ebel Theater, it quickly became clear that, in the aftermath of the Winter Olympics he would remain intransigent in his publicly expressed loathing of expensive snow games. He especially attacked the luge. "Is there any sport where you do LESS?" he raged from the stage. "And what about those speed skaters?" He mimed their cross-legged ice-swaying. "Frog-people!" he cried viciously, scorning their bulky thighs. Let's fact it: Billy

dislikes pretty well any sport that does not involve green
and white jerseys, a football and two goal posts.

There was a small party in the balcony reception area
after the show. It was an eclectic gathering, with
conversation to match. A colleague from my clinical
world, Dr Hamlin Emory, had turned up. I sometimes
wonder just how my fellow professionals will take my
husband, since he is so . . . unusual . . . but in this case
I needn't have worried.

"Your husband's remarkable," he enthused with a
soupçon of terror. "It was like witnessing a wonderful
archaeological excavation taking place in loamy
aromatic soil. The word-shards he finds are delicious!
And he speaks in the idiom that existed prior to the
Great Vowel Shift. He would enjoy Aristotle . . . I'm
going to send him some stuff." Ignoring the bemused
expressions of more street-smart people around him, he
continued with escalating passion: "Brave man!
Profound! He should do a review of polytheism. I'm in
complete agreement with him, of course: 'God' is a
nominalistic fallacy!"

Nearby, one of Amy's school chums delivered a
contrasting accolade in the language of cool:

"Dude . . . your dad rocks!" he slow-mumbled.
"That was tight!"

Football team members filed in, beautiful, tight-
muscled men with shiny skin and chic, gelled hair.

"Wow," said Billy in my ear. I expected to hear he
was impressed by their prowess on the field. "Did you
notice they're all wearing Prada?" he said, which left
me wondering how on earth he knew that. My husband

among the Italian designer cognoscenti. I love that he constantly surprises me.

People all around us continued to buzz with après-show reruns and remembrances.

"Now I know what younger British comics were watching when they were growing up," remarked one man.

"Loved the thing about the seven-foot-tall woman dragging a dialysis machine," said another, referring to Billy's latest comments about the elusiveness of Bin Laden.

"I came in late," a fashion guru apologised to me. "It was dark but I saw you sitting at the back."

"That wasn't me," I explained, "that was Darryl Hannah, the tall willowy blonde. I'm the short dumpy one."

Billy continued to decimate winter sports for that entire series of concerts. By the Saturday night, his comments about speed skating had become a mightily extended "frog-people" mime-and-rant that lasted twenty minutes. He had perfected the minimalist, in-sled deportment of an Olympic-standard lugist and people just screamed. It seems to me that in America, as in other parts of the world, Billy has become something of a comedians' comedian, and an actors' one as well. The shows in Los Angeles were more than ever stuffed with luminaries sliding under their seats. "It's like Oscar night," said a nineteen-year-old in a *Terminator* T-shirt.

The following day, which was a relaxing no-concert one for Billy, a dozen pals who'd attended the previous night's show gathered at our house for Sunday brunch. After omelettes, fruit salad and a discussion of current anti-terrorism security measures in the city's film studios, the conversation turned to reminiscing about Elvis Presley.

"This guy Tony was employed to hang around Elvis's house to play piano whenever Elvis felt like singing," announced Danny Ferrington, the world's greatest guitar-maker. Danny is a sweet, self-effacing man with the sensibility of an ebullient child. His high-pitched Southern drawl can dominate any room.

"Elvis would be just lying on the couch for hours . . . then all of a sudden there would be this deep crooning . . ." Danny imitated The King emerging from a sound sleep with rhythm on his brain, "and Tony would have to spring to the piano, find the right key, and accompany him wherever his vocal fancy took him. See . . ." Danny glanced conspiratorially around the room . . . "I guess the only time Elvis was ever truly happy was when he was singing."

I glanced at Billy, expecting him to acknowledge some sense of commonality in the story, for sometimes I think that's true of my husband and his comedy, but he was off on his own track.

"Elvis couldn't use a knife and fork," Billy mused. "He'd been brought up on burgers and hot dogs, so he never learned the niceties of cutlery. Avoided restaurants like the plague."

How did he know that? True or not, I was astonished by this bon mot, coming from a man who, at our very first meal together, ate fish with his bare hands. The

41

notion that he perceived Elvis to be so much lower down than he on the barbarism scale was so delightfully ridiculous I must have been eyeing him with disbelief.

"Whattt?" Billy spat out the word in my direction, while everyone else chortled into their coffee. The previous night most of the present company had heard him on stage referring to the tendency of "women" to ask a question with a look . . . to which he says the male riposte is invariably the same . . . a defensive "Whattt?"

Billy would shortly have even more reason to use the word for that very afternoon, with the faint, halting tones of Scarlett's flute practice in the background, I decided it was time to drop my first hint about throwing him a birthday party. Not just any old cheery gathering, but a seriously lavish celebration of his life so far. The idea seemed to terrify him, and it was not hard to work out why. In order for him to allow himself to be fêted on such a grand scale Billy would have to accept the as yet unthinkable: that everyone felt he deserved it. For a man who had always been told he was useless and would never amount to anything, it would be a gargantuan step to concede such a notion, and the ancient voices inside his head said "you're unworthy". Then there was the prospect of being faced with undeniable proof that he was turning sixty, not an easy task for even the most chronologically comfortable among us.

"It would be fun," I coaxed, after being met with a barrage of negativity.

We were a long way from agreeing on this subject, and I could tell it was going to be a tough road. As the conversation reached an impasse, Billy found an interesting way to gain the upper hand:

"Did I tell you," he said, deliberately changing the subject, "that next month I'm going to be doing a naked Roman orgy scene with scantily clad women for a TV commercial?"

"No," I replied coolly. "You hadn't mentioned that."

Billy may have it in for frog-people, but he has long cherished genuine amphibians. As a youngster, he loved to happen upon frogspawn in Glasgow's Botanic Gardens, where there were a series of small ponds containing slimy plant and animal life. He'd collect it in a jam jar and stick it on the kitchen windowsill. Billy thought frogspawn was dynamite stuff, and monitored its progress with fascination as the black spot morphed first into a tadpole and then a baby frog. He had to watch carefully for the exact moment just before the creatures were mobile enough to climb out of their glass playpen so he could promptly return them to their home in the pond. Otherwise there'd be hell to pay, with frogs all over the kitchen or plummeting to their deaths off the window ledge.

It was a surprise to me to hear that as a child Billy actually took himself on nature appreciation walks in the middle of Glasgow. Nature was alive and well in the excellent public parks that were established throughout the inner city, and Billy loved, for example, to pick leaf buds and watch them develop. Nowadays he thinks buds are stunning things to show children. "I feel sorry for kids who are brought up without finding out that those sticky wee burrs are great to throw at people's backs," he says. "Beats the shit out of SpongeBob SquarePants." It has not been easy for Billy to watch his children grow up with such different experiences from him; and at the same time that has occasionally been disconcerting for his children. When Billy's daughter Cara was five years old, she was taken by her grandfather on an outing to the Barrows market in Glasgow:

"Dad . . . we've got to get a bus," she said excitedly when she returned. "They're brilliant!"

"But we've got a Mercedes," he said proudly. "Great car!"

"No, but," she insisted, "a bus would be much more fun. You can go upstairs on them and look in people's houses and see them watching TV and everything!"

Like most parents, Billy is sometimes hard-pressed by ambivalent feelings about how exactly to be a father. On the one hand he wants to provide his children with all the material gifts he never had, yet he also suspects that character deficits can accompany affluence. In addition to that, people who have not had good parents have to work a lot harder than others to raise their children well. The distant echoes of over-harsh, over-indulgent or disconnected voices lie treacherously in the mind's eye, waiting for a moment to be perpetrated upon one's own children. It requires great vigilance to be able to arrest, quieten and change such insistent phantoms. Fortunately, Billy has the necessary

44

awareness. Moreover, he loves all his children most deeply, and they fully know it.

But sometimes I am rudely reminded that culturally, Billy is shockingly different from most people we come across outside Scotland. On Billy's next concert break, five days later, we were hosts to a group of fellow school parents whose children were due to visit us for a weekend stay. I suppose parents all over the world like to meet the parents of their children's friends, if only to vet them as supervisors of their own children when they go over to play. We gathered in one of the newer Hollywood restaurants, all chrome chic and Chardonnay. These were sophisticated people from diverse backgrounds who were quite unused to the Glaswegian language and sensibilities: a CEO, a lawyer, an arts administrator. Over the *risotto funghi* with just a hint of basil, Billy got on a roll, for some unknown reason deciding to discuss his tendency to perform violent acts towards paparazzi, ornery journalists, and anyone else who gets in his face. I became quieter and quieter as I assessed the effect of this Glasgow hard-man fighting talk on such an elegant coterie. There was no doubt about it: the atmosphere was definitely becoming a tad strained. Finally I could take it no more.

"Darling," I said firmly, attempting light-heartedness, "these good people are about to entrust their children to us for a sleep-over with Daisy on Saturday night . . ."

Billy looked at me with an expression of utter bewilderment.

"What are you talking about?"

I struggled to formulate an explanation.

"Well, just as long as there won't be any paparazzi there," muttered one brave father.

One can never be quite sure how Billy will be received by teachers and school officials either. The next day we had a worrying call from the school's administrative office.

"The Principal would like to see Mr Connolly."

It sounded ominous, so at 4p.m. promptly I accompanied Billy to the inner sanctum waiting room. We sat there nervously speculating about which of our children was most likely to be facing expulsion, and were eventually ushered into an untidy office, rich with files, framed certificates and exploding filing cabinets.

"Ah, Mr Connolly." The Principal, in jeans and checked shirt, looked far more laid-back than his British counterparts, but he was nevertheless a grey man with a harried air.

"I'd like you to take a look at something," he announced sternly. Billy and I exchanged glances. "Oh God," we thought, "he's got evidence."

He reached behind him to an over-stacked book shelf, and pulled out a prized, leatherbound volume. He rustled through it impatiently for a moment, then presented the open pages to Billy with a flourish.

"Read that, please!"

Still charged with adrenalin, Billy took the proffered book and peered at the page.

"'Holy Willie's Prayer' by Robert Burns," he read out loud, throwing the scholar a very old-fashioned look. The Principal nodded enthusiastically for him to

46

continue, and leaned forward expectantly in his chair with hands clasped. As our pulses returned to resting mode, we grasped that for a literary aficionado stuck in Southern California, this was the treat of a lifetime: a Burns poem finally read with the proper accent.

Billy has never got used to the school system as it is experienced in the California society where our teenagers go to school. It's a place where children are respected and encouraged to speak their minds, a far cry from the atmosphere of daily batterings, moral oppression, and the "don't question the teacher", spoon-feeding approach he knew as a youngster in Glasgow.

Billy is amazed at his children's attitude towards it.

"I can't believe it," he said to me once. "They actually *like* school!"

It is fascinating to watch him talk with his children about the encouragement they are given to freely express themselves in class. It's a teaching style that stuns him.

"What?" Billy will cry incredulously. "The teacher asked *you* for *your opinion?*"

It's not just the empowerment of children at school that baffles him. I've caught him gazing in amazement at billboards for "Childline", the telephone help resource for mistreated youngsters. For him, the very idea of a child having some power to redress abuse is astonishing, given his own early sense of hopelessness. For him there had been no way out.

The middle-classness of his fellow school parents is also a challenge for Billy, as are the parent-teacher conferences. I sometimes have to intervene to prevent the latter becoming Billy Connolly stand-up sessions, with screeching teachers and little talk of grades. I'm always afraid he'll swear, which is more a reflection of my own morally repressive schooling, in a Church of England girls' grammar school, than of any real potential for repercussions. For Billy, swearing is innate and it seems to run in the family. He has been happily cursing away since he was three years old. His son James also swore from very early on, so much so that his parents carried a plastic fork around with them so they could pretend he was asking for it whenever he said "fuck" in polite company.

There was far less tolerance for using four-letter words among some of Billy's more religious relatives. At five years old, his little cousin used one at her family dinner table.

"Oh fuck," she exclaimed.

There was dead silence. Billy's uncle laid down his knife and fork.

"That's a very interesting word. What do you think it means?"

She thought for a second or two.

"I think it means the dinner's rotten."

CHAPTER
THREE

Seeing My Own
Spotty Arse

It was a rare chance for dancing in Drumchapel. Glorious live band music emanated from the wooden building beside St Lawrence's church, the only Catholic place of worship in the whole area. Eager seventeen-year-olds were arriving from the surrounding suburbs, throwing off their coats on to a messy pile and pushing their way into the lively crowd of Catholic youths already on the dance floor. Huddled outside in the shadows with several Protestant friends, Billy rehearsed them one last time.

"Hail Mary, Full of Grace . . ."

One of them was either a very slow learner, or else that bucket of cider he'd downed on the bus was taking its toll. He looked quite pasty, and Billy wondered if it was worth the effort. They had a little arrangement, him and the guys. If they sneaked him into the Protestant dances in Glasgow, he made sure they had a chance with the Catholic girls of Drumchapel. The priest had announced the dance at Mass the previous Sunday.

"I'd like to encourage you young people to attend," he smiled enthusiastically from the pulpit, "so you may meet with other Catholic youth . . ."

He did not say that Protestants were unwelcome, but Billy had heard that non-Catholic suspects could be challenged to a prayer. The Lord's Prayer would be a dead giveaway, and any interloper who stupidly spouted it would be hauled off by his earlobe.

Billy wished his friend and fellow welding apprentice Joe West was there to help teach the prayers. Joe knew the ropes about most things. He'd already taught Billy to dress, smoke and drink, and was now coaching him on how to get girls to dance with him without risking excessive humiliation.

"Right, that's it. We're going in." Billy was sick of all this effort. "And mind you remember to cross yourself when you pass the crucifix."

"I'm no well," complained the lad with a belly full of cider.

They waited impatiently while he vomited on a rose bed of winter thorns, then charged into the hall like a Wild West posse off to plunder a train.

Inside, a group of musicians called The Dominos were playing a slow number. Billy thought them much better than the Protestant bands, who, although impressive in their ability to play "The Sash My Father Wore" in any rhythm, whether waltz, foxtrot, even tango, nevertheless knew little of Perry Como. He wished there was jiving, but in this hall only ballroom and slow dancing were allowed. The larger commercial ballrooms always had a Jivers' Corner, but here in the wee church hall they weren't taking any chances that people might crash into one another. That was bound to start a fight.

Billy sashayed over to the perimeter of the dance floor. Joe had taught him to lurk on the side until two girls who were dancing together came closer. He would then begin to dance alone near the prettiest one, hoping she would turn to him and abandon her friend. Billy's eyes sifted though the mass of dancers like a neophyte marksman planning a hit. Gauche and spotty boys were twirling with lanky, short-haired girls; more developed young ladies in swing skirts hung coyly on the shoulders of the taller boys in mohair suits, while unattached youths like him skulked uneasily on the periphery. Suddenly, he noticed a couple of girls attempting an unauthorised conservative jive step off to his left. He ventured towards them for a better look, and as he did so his heart began to beat a little faster. A pretty fair-haired girl wearing a tight-fitting cream jersey and a red skirt with lipstick to match was dancing with an extremely large, plain brunette in a frumpy polka-dot dress with flounced petticoats. Perfect situation. He steered purposefully towards the blonde.

Miraculously, she behaved as if she knew him, and smiled warmly, beckoning him over to her.

"Brilliant," thought Billy, checking his collar, "I must be getting the hang of this. She's obviously dying to dance with me . . . and I didn't even need Joe's help."

Elated, he waved back. He swaggered over to her with a triumphant air, preparing his arms to surround

51

her for slow dancing. When he was practically touching her, however, she slithered out of his grasp, ducked behind him, and pushed him slap into her plain friend's arms. It was a move that had been practised a hundred times before.

"I'll see you around," smiled the blonde, grabbing a cocky older boy who'd been waiting for her at a nearby table.

"That's it," cooed her friend, wrenching him closer with a gummy smile. "Dance with Big Agnes . . ."

Billy has made up for his early ineptness with women in ways that, as a lad, he never would have believed possible. In March, for example, he actually did engage in a naked Roman orgy with scantily clad women. It was a scene for a television commercial for the Camelot lottery. His whole body was painted gold.

"What are they calling it?" I asked nervously. "Boldfinger?"

"It was nothing wonderful." He down-played it when he returned. "But the body-paint looked great with my beard. Purple and gold go very well together."

"Indeed," I said watching him unpack. "So, luscious maidens were draped all over you?" It's a wife's duty to be just a little suspicious.

"Mmm," he demurred. "I'll get a lot of stick from people when it comes out: 'Saw your fat arse again. Why don't you put your clothes on?' That kind of thing."

"Did you have anything on?"

"I had a wee piece of bum floss holding things together."

"So . . . tell me about the scene . . ." This was difficult.

"We were . . . reclining. I was doing the talking. They were just being . . . grapey. I only spoke to them when absolutely necessary, as in 'God, my arse is numb. Mind if I move?' It was the same when I did that Sharon Stone movie where I was thrashing around with two beautiful naked mud wrestlers. Most of the time I was saying: 'I can't fucking see. My eyes are full of mud.'"

"Wait a minute." This was the first I'd heard of that. I had actually never seen *Beautiful Joe*. "You were mud wrestling with two naked women?"

"Well," he folded a T-shirt, "I *think* they were naked. Soft things were sliding all over me, but I was never sure which bits they were."

That put an end to my mini inquisition, for it made me shriek with laughter. I can never interrogate Billy for very long, because he always comes out with something that pops my cork.

"Did you know," he said, compounding my helplessness, "that over the years three women have vomited on me?"

"Three?" I had heard him talk hilariously about two of them on stage. "That's too many for all of them to be purely accidental." I found myself conducting a scientific enquiry. "Was there a common attribute? Did you instigate their biliousness in any particular way?"

"Well, I guess I have that disposable fucking look about me," he conceded.

"Nonsense," I laughed. Billy still doesn't think he's handsome, no matter how much I compliment him. "And I don't know why you're unpacking. You're off to New York tomorrow."

We sipped peppermint tea after dinner, roaring at *The Phil Hendrie Show* on the radio. Phil phones into his own show as other characters, and even interviews himself. He lures innocent people to call up to complain about his (faked) bigotry and the whole thing gets quite brilliantly out-of-hand. Afterwards, when Billy and I were both relaxed, it seemed like a rare opportunity to revisit the subject of the big birthday party.

"I don't fancy it," he said, still quite fearful. "We should do something very small."

"Like what?" I said. "It's a really important occasion and everyone we know will want to be part of it."

"That's the problem," he replied, quite sensibly. "How many people could we possibly invite?"

"We could have it at Candacraig," I said. "Maybe in the garden."

"Outside? At the end of November? Are you kidding me?"

"No," I said, "we should do it before your actual birthday, in the summer. Then we can have a smaller celebration on your actual birthday."

"An official birthday party?" He laughed at the idea. "What, like the Queen?"

"Uh huh," I said, "except by contrast you'll be carrying out a Trooping of the Beige."

But even my suggestion that instead of Sexagesimus we rename it his *Sexageniality* did not assuage his ambivalence about the prospect. In fact, it transpired that Billy was quite doubtful that there was any sex or geniality to be had at all after the age of sixty. In common with many other people who are influenced by popular mythology, he even wondered if he would continue to be passionate, as if just having a birthday could suddenly turn him off like a bath tap.

"Pamsy, did you hear about the man who found a frog under his bed?" As usual, Billy had found a joke that matched his personal zeitgeist. "He was about to squish it when it cried, 'Stop! I'm a frog with special talents. If you give me a kiss I can arrange for you to have any sexual experience you desire.' But the man picked up the frog and put it in his pocket. 'Let me out!' yelled the frog. 'No,' replied the man. 'You don't understand,' pleaded the frog, 'you can have any sex you want . . . anything . . . exotic stuff . . . ANYTHING . . . just kiss me!' 'Nope,' replied the man. 'I'm sixty years old. At my age it's more useful to have a talking frog.'"

I didn't laugh. "That's all rubbish," I said, failing to avoid a "professional advice" tone of voice. "Just getting older doesn't automatically mean the end of sexual desire . . . or ability."

"Thank God for that," he said, exhaling, "'cos I was only just getting good at it."

I looked at him with new curiosity.

I have always thought my husband very comfortable with his body, both its anatomy and physiology. Only a man who was confident about every bit of his physique would run about naked in public as much as he does. His physical appearance has even been immortalised in Madame Tussaud's Wax Museum in London. Billy thinks they did an excellent job, far better than a previous attempt by someone in Edinburgh, who apparently dressed a reject Elvis Presley body in the black tights and banana boots my husband was once known for and added a Billy Connolly head. When Billy went to see it, he found it wanting in the crotch department.

"I look like a woman down there," he objected.

"Och, well, we'll have to measure you again," said the wax worker.

"No thanks," said Billy. "Just add a nice bulge. I could suggest a packet of birthday candles, if you're a bit short of wax."

With a series of New York concerts ahead of him, Billy set off on a warm Californian afternoon to catch the red-eye to John F. Kennedy airport. He was wearing a pair of denim cowboy boots, jeans with buttons down the sides, and a T-shirt with *One Love One Law* written across his chest.

"Billy," I said, "um . . . according to CNN it's still winter in New York." I was packing thermals for my arrival there the following day.

"Good," he said happily, not taking the hint. "There'll be skaters at the Rockefeller Center. See you."

Considering Billy's current state of mind, it seemed quite unfair that on the plane, he was seated near a certain successful young male actor with whom he'd worked in the past.

"I'm knackered," said the man, downing a beer.

"Why, what's up with you?" asked Billy.

"All these women," he replied. "It's been two or three a day in LA."

"Am I supposed to feel sorry for you?" replied Billy, muttering "Prick!" under his breath and burying his nose in *Gormenghast* for the rest of the flight.

On the night of Billy's first gig at the Town Hall, a three-thousand-seater venue he always thoroughly enjoyed, he was still jacketless, so he took a cab four blocks. At exactly the same time, unbeknown to him, I was just arriving at JFK, having managed to get on an earlier flight than I'd planned. It was rush hour in Manhattan, and traffic was gridlocked right around 57th Street. A large tourist bus sat in the middle of it all, barring the passage of many commuters. As Billy sat there he noticed a particularly aggrieved businessman beside him in a Pontiac, ineffectually honking his horn as if that could move the thoroughly wedged vehicle. As he continued to watch, the man got out of his car and slammed his door. He then walked up to the open windows of the bus, leaned in and shouted "Go fuck yourselves!" to all the tourists sitting quietly in their seats doing no harm to anyone. Then the man about-turned and got calmly back in his car. Billy began to absolutely howl at the silliness, the ineffectiveness, and the downright effrontery of the man. He got out of the cab and began to walk to the theatre, sporadically bursting into laughter as he re-ran the event in his mind. He was still laughing about it when he walked on stage.

"That guy's my hero," Billy told his audience. It's the benign aspect of the victims that always makes him cry with mirth.

As far as Billy's concerned, New York is the Glasgow of North America, and the moment he got onstage, he felt like he was home. The crowd was to his liking, the shape of the room suited him, and he went flying. In the spotlight's edge that spilled over the front row, he noticed a man in a kilt. The vast majority of his New York audience is American but, due to the early New World immigration of Irish and Scottish people, many who live there have common ancestry with Billy. One man he met said his mother lived in Pollock, a housing estate between Glasgow and Paisley.

"Pollock?" said Billy. "My granny used to live there."

"Yeah . . . I went there once," shrugged the man. "Drove around. Weird place, man . . . there were cars on fire and everything."

Old-time variety artists used to begin sentences with "Take my wife," sometimes followed by "*Please* take my wife". Billy was echoing that particular sentiment just as I arrived backstage. "Now, my wife is a very clever person . . ."

Such a sentence, if uttered by Billy during a performance, can be very ominous for me. I was just entering his dressing room, a couch-lined retreat with the remains of a cold buffet wilting under the scorching glare of hundred-watt bulb mirror lights, when I heard him say it over the relay speakers. Knowing exactly what was in store for me, Steve Brown and Malcolm Kingsnorth, his manager and sound engineer, exchanged anticipatory smirks. As Billy's on-stage self-disclosure seeped into the dressing room, I struggled to avoid their gaze.

"But I'm a kind of a plain man, sexually speaking. I'm not into exotic sex, dressing up and all that . . ."

I was thinking of exiting the room, but that would only have drawn attention to my discomfort. I had no idea where he was going with this.

"I mean," he continued, "I don't do that sort of thing. I don't last long enough for any of that. And what would I need a ceiling mirror for? Puts me off, seeing my own spotty arse . . ."

"Anyone want a cup of tea?"

Embarrassment was upon me again. I just never know what Billy's going to say in his show that might accurately or otherwise implicate me, and I quite often have to avoid eye-contact when the lights come up. It occurred to me he might talk more about me on stage when he thought I was not in the audience, for he is a considerate man. I should probably attend more often, because people are always giving me funny looks the next day, and I never know quite what it's about.

It was a brilliant show. I had wondered if a post-September 11th New York audience would be ready for his highly topical political ranting, but he pitched it just right and won them instantly. He left the theatre with a happy, satisfied après-show glow, and a lot warmer in

59

the jacket I had brought him. With the subway steam swirling around us, we ate pretzels in the street on the way back to the hotel, while the thundering city slowed down for the night.

"I never would have thought you'd get away with all that stuff about terrorism here," I said.

"Och," he shrugged. "You must go for it."

"Did you see that guy in the front row wearing a kilt?"

"Yes I did," he said. "I found it strangely comforting."

At 7th Avenue we saw that a taxi and a Chevrolet had collided. The two drivers were arguing from inside their cars without even bothering to get out. "Why don't you sleep at home, you motherfucker?" yelled the taxi driver, causing Billy to collapse on a street lamp.

I am thankful that, after a performance, Billy is usually far less angst-ridden than many other comedians I've known. In my own former life as a comedian, I certainly fell into the category of the over-analytic comic. Naturally given to harsh self-criticism, it was torturous to anticipate performing live, and even worse afterwards, although I enjoyed those moments when I was actually in front of an audience. In Billy's opinion, the luckiest people in the world are those who do what they should be doing. "Doing what you love's where happiness is," says Billy. "It's the ultimate paycheque." He hit the haggis on the head.

As a psychologist now, I'm thankful to be doing something that gives me great satisfaction. Moreover, it does not involve working with Indian rock pythons, which was one of the least enjoyable aspects of my previous career. After I had spent several years working in television comedy on both sides of the Atlantic Ocean, I decided to develop a solo show to take on the road around Britain, Australia, New Zealand and the Arab Emirates. For reasons that I can no longer even remember, the show ended up being not so much a solo show, but a whole company that comprised me, two dwarfs and a snake. Melanie and Tony (the "little people" as dwarfs prefer to be called) were delightful and professional additions to the show; however, the python was a whole other story.

Fred, as the annoying reptile was known, was frequently in semi-hibernation and had to be woken for the show by draping him around the dressing-room mirror where the lights provided the necessary warmth to arouse him. It was, however, his digestive processes that made him an insufferable stage mate. Fred was uninterested in processed pet food. He ate a quarter of a sheep every month, immediately after which he digested the food in a most antisocial fashion, leaving puddles of snake excrement all over the stage. And let me tell you one other titbit that may have thus far escaped your notice: if you're alone on stage with a snake that farts, nobody thinks it's the snake.

The following day we headed for the New York Museum of Modern Art. We usually pay MoMA a visit whenever we're there, because it's always inspiring. When I was in the process of changing my career, and feeling quite fearful of doing so, I went to the Henri Matisse retrospective. It was interesting to see his early

61

work, unremarkable still-life paintings and portraits, followed by his development through the years to creating the extraordinary work for which he is known. When I got as far as the rooms in which his most brilliant work was hung, such as *Music* and my favourite, his psychologically intense work *The Conversation*, I was so affected by it I considered retracing my steps rather than continuing on to witness what I imagined would be his decline. But around the next corner of the exhibition I found *Jazz*, the stunning cutouts in which he achieved such movement, vibrant colour and vitality. I could hardly believe that the man did his most dynamic, sexy work in his seventies. Discovering that even such a celebrated artist as Matisse was unafraid to abandon painting and take up collage in his last decade when he was ill and bedridden, had a profound influence on both Billy and me. It provided enormous encouragement during my time of transition and I hoped Billy would remember it as he moved into his sixties.

Despite our love of MoMA, both Billy and I tend to become overstimulated and overwhelmed by such a concentration of extraordinary art. We were both tired that day so, when we arrived at the bright and bustling glass-canopied structure and saw the long queues, it was almost with relief that we agreed to bail out. We bought the girls "Crumpled Paper" trompe l'oeil stationery in the gift shop, then went instead to an exhibition of photographs taken by ordinary citizens on September 11th. They were shocking visual diaries of that day, taken from windows, balconies, and crouched positions in the ash-covered streets. As with great paintings, snapshots that capture raw human pain are also overwhelming. We walked back to the hotel in silence, hand in hand, utterly thankful for our blessed lives.

I flew back to Los Angeles the following day and found that, not surprisingly, both home and office work had been piling up. Like many women, I find the juggling of home and career requirements to be extremely challenging, not to mention trying to keep up with my nomadic husband. There were lectures to prepare, dogs to de-flea, and teenagers to keep in line. As it happened, I saw fit to ground one of the latter for a serious curfew violation. After hearing her sentence she marched off petulantly and turned on the TV, and was immediately confronted by the profoundly shocking sight of her mother (albeit from a breakfast television show twenty years before), removing a bewildered man's pants. That chance sighting rather took the edge off my effectiveness as a disciplinarian for quite some time.

It was a relief when Billy came home at the end of the month.

"Let's all go out to dinner to celebrate," he called to the girls.

"I'll be there in a minute," I said, opening an email containing analysed research material. "I'm just downloading one hundred and sixty-four histograms."

"I think there's a cure for that," he said. "Calcium, I believe."

The next day he turned up at my professional waiting room to meet me for sushi a few minutes early. Two women were sitting together when he arrived, waiting to see a colleague. Billy glanced around the ivory wallpapered suite-entrance, restfully decorated with natural-fibre collages and well-tended orchid plants, and plonked himself down opposite the pair. They had an air of apprehension about them, which aroused his curiosity. Being a friendly chap, not to mention brave of mouth, Billy decided to ignore the unwritten code of behaviour for such a situation and strike up a conversation.

"What are you two here for?" he asked, not pulling any punches.

After they recovered from the shock of being asked such an impertinent question, they informed him that they were having a problem with their relationship.

"Ah!" he said. "Lesbians, eh?"

If only I could have intervened right then and there.

"No," one replied, quite acidly. "She's my sister-in-law and we have our differences. We're here to try to sort them out."

"Fat chance," said the other. You could slice the atmosphere with a kilt pin.

Billy thought for a minute or two, then came up with a brilliant idea.

"Well," he enquired, "what makes you think you have to get on? Couldn't you simply agree to disagree? Couldn't you just say fuck it, we're always going to have our differences?"

There was a long pause while the two women thought this through. Finally they looked at each other with the wide-eyed realisation that there was a sage in the room, and what's more he was free of charge. They were just creeping out of the waiting room when my colleague came through and stopped them. Fortunately, she saw the funny side. I have, however, thought about banning him from my office.

The next morning at breakfast, Billy seemed unusually contrite about the previous day's debacle. He made a surprising announcement.

"I've been trying to become less weird." He was stirring his tea with a fluffy ruler.

"Is it working?" volunteered Amy after a pregnant silence.

"I don't think so," he replied. "I can tell by the way people look at me when I offer them my profound ramblings. They stare at me as if one of my eyes has just dropped out."

I quickly altered my own fixed expression and changed the subject.

"Did you know," I said, reading a psychiatric journal, "that there's a medication with a particularly interesting side effect: sneezing can trigger involuntary orgasm."

Billy is rather pleased that one of my psychological specialities is human sexuality because he finds great humour in it. He was delighted with this snippet and couldn't wait to make the most of it in his very next public appearance. I tuned in to a chat show just in time to see him saying, "So he told his friend about his propensity to orgasm while sneezing. The friend asked if he was taking anything for it. 'Yeah,' said the guy, 'pepper.'"

Occasionally, Billy even tries to blind me with my own science.

"I was reading," he announced as March came to an end, "that there's a thing lives in your eyelash that's got two penises. I don't know what the Latin name is but the translation's *lucky bastard*."

CHAPTER
FOUR

Inserting The Bumkin
From Aft

"Wool is a bugger of a thing," thought Billy, at six years old. The dark blue woollen beret his aunt had jammed on his head itched his forehead worse than a swarm of midges. He was not to remove it on pain of a sore thrashing, so he scratched the skin around it until it was red-raw. He envied his friend Vinny Maron, marching beside him in a plastic trenchcoat with a fine matching belt and wellies, as they headed for Kelvingrove Park. Their older sisters, Florence and Margaret, flounced ahead of them, all secrets, giggles, and pubescent longings.

It was a crisp spring Saturday. The parks were alive with daffodils, but the wind still felt cruel to the pond-hopping four. They had already caught bagaminnies in the well-loved Victoria Park pond in Whiteinch, a magnet for toy-boat sailors, both children and adults alike. Two years earlier, Billy had made boats with paper and pencils that he could sail in puddles, but now he had a glorious, ten-inch wooden yacht that his father brought him back when he returned from the war. On this occasion, though, he'd left it behind, probably because of all the kerfuffle over his beret. There was a wooden shed beside the pond where people could store larger boats. You could peek though cracks in the wall and see astounding beauties with real canvas sails and working ropes, some of them as much as six feet tall when fully rigged. Now that spring was here, cloth-capped men in shirtsleeves would cycle down to the pond after work to sail them at twilight, using rubber-tipped poles to shove them confidently out into the wind.

At last, the foursome reached the waist-high walled pond in Kelvingrove Park, with its splendidly ornate, polished granite fountain, a Victorian fantasy of carved swans, exotic birds, and intricate pockets through which the water could cascade. This was not usually a place for sailing boats, but they decided to improvise. The four of them leaned excitedly over the marble bank, legs in the air, and began to float the little orange peel domes they'd saved from their packed lunches. They launched them out with sticks as far as they could, then watched anxiously as the elements took control.

Florence's bobbed merrily in the wake of a large plastic cutter, but Vinny's was heading for a waterfall that would surely capsize it, so he leaned a little further out from the edge to try to alter its course. With his legs flailing about in the air and nothing to hold on to, the marble pond surround became a slippery slide, allowing him to slither over the polished stone as gracefully as a seal and land in the water with a plop. His trenchcoat floated up to the surface before he did.

"Billy Connolly! You pushed him in!" cried Margaret, running towards him.

Before Billy had a chance to defend himself he felt a thwacking hand on his shoulder and then splash-contact with freezing, murky water as it covered his own body. He emerged considerably heavier than he went in, since his thick woollen clothing absorbed its weight in water. He had to be dragged out by Florence and two passing shop girls before the sodden boys were frog-marched home forthwith.

"We're all going to catch it!" moaned Florence, but that was the least of their worries. She and Margaret were so busy arguing about whose fault it was that they failed to notice the most immediate problem, which was that Billy could no longer see. His beret had slipped over his eyes and shrunk when it hit water, and was now firmly stuck on his nose. Everyone tried to extract it, including the ice-cream vendor, but in the end they had to lead him blind, wailing and wet through the streets of Glasgow to their inevitable fate.

"You bunch of eejits!" his father stormed. He had to cut it off with a pair of scissors.

Considering this soggy debacle, it is somewhat surprising that sailing boats now remind Billy of gentle, quiet pleasure. As an older schoolboy, he frequently crossed the River Clyde to get to his school, St Gerard's. He had a ticket for the underground, but preferred the smell and gaiety of flags and funnels and

69

ships. He never managed to board one until his uncle Mick became a steward on a popular vessel-turned-nightclub called *The Carrick*. Standing there on its fairy-lit deck, with Dean Martin background music and the smell of stale beer, cigarettes and sausages, he could almost imagine he was ocean bound, happily rolling somewhere between Bombay and Baltimore, or Cairo and the Cape.

The Carrick was moored on the Broomielaw, a city dock at the bottom of Stockwell Street. Billy was amazed to learn that it was right there that his Irish ancestors first encountered the streets of Glasgow. They had disembarked weary, sick and starving, to pick potatoes in the Scottish countryside.

> *Wha' saw the tattie hawkers*
> *Wha' saw them gang awa'*
> *Wha' saw the tattie hawkers*
> *Gangin' doon the Broomielaw*

Billy still just loves everything about the River Clyde. Throughout his boyhood he watched great vessels glide out of its harbour, and plotted his own escape. Giants with iron-stained hulls and cloud-kissing funnels were waiting to take him to places every Glasgow schoolboy has considered: America, China, Africa, Spain. The world was out there.

As Billy grew into a man, his fascination with the sea grew even stronger. He was never drawn to being *in* the sea, though, just on top of it. Billy believes the toothy, predatory monsters of the deep are there to remind us that humans have no right to venture into their world. He is even ambivalent about bobbing about on its surface, since he is apt to feel queasy in the calmest waters. No, it is the *romance* of the sea that has tugged at his heart since boyhood, a Conradesque fantasy of adventure, escape and exotic women. Billy has never read *The Sea* by Joseph Conrad (one of my favourites) yet it utterly reflects his mariner soul.

It was hardly surprising, therefore, that Billy decided that April to establish a home in Malta, a windswept, seafaring place. The islands' magnificent coastlines have seen hell-bent Turkish warships, sinister pirate ships, a slaving vessel or two, and the French man o' war.

"Every marauding army, on its way to conquer others, stopped off and practised on the Maltese." Billy has it all figured out. "The captain would say, 'Let the soldiers off the boat, beat the shit out of anyone you meet, and if you don't want to do that, marry someone local and have a couple of children.'"

Nowadays the local sea craft are far less threatening: jaunty fishing boats with square cabins and turquoise decks, sporty little cruisers, open dinghies with yellow-rimmed blue hulls and white-and-red trim, and the monstrous white Channel car ferry designed for the scores of day-trippers who hop between the main landforms.

The Maltese islands form a breezy, limestone archipelago, smack in the middle of the southern Mediterranean Sea. Malta's reputation among the British as a down-market holiday destination hardly does it justice, for it is a fascinating intersection of European and Middle Eastern cultures, with a rich and surprising history. Billy and I are captivated by the diversity of the culture, a mixture of African, European and Levantine influences. Its people are of Phoenician descent, and speak an essentially Semitic language with Arab influence. Billy of course has sorted out the class differences. "The upper class sound more Italian, and the working class sound more Arab," he decided. Billy is a recent recipient of an Honorary Doctorate of Letters from Glasgow University, but his passion for language is longstanding. He was delighted to hear that Edward Lear invented new words to describe Gozo, the second largest island, and site of Homer's fabled Calypso's Cave. "Its scenery," wrote Lear in 1866, "may truly be called pomskizillious and gromphibberous, being as no words can describe its magnificence."

Our most absorbing new challenge is trying to pronounce Maltese words like "*xlendi*" or "*xlokk*". The latter is the name for a hot, humid wind that deposits rust-red Sahara sand on every single surface, even indoors. It is intriguing to imagine where those fine grains last lay; beneath camel-hooves, Berber tent, or blue-dyed toes of Tuareg men.

Billy is not an acquisitive person (apart from his banjo, snow globe and cowboy boot collection), but he couldn't resist buying the 1930s Catholic schoolhouse that had been transformed into a Maltese palazzo. For a while I was opposed to the purchase, until it dawned on me that, for Billy, this was an exquisite act of revenge, a symbolic triumph over every sadistic brute of a teacher who beat him for his inattention. Once the former place of learning had been emptied, gutted, scraped and scrubbed, I set to work replacing hardwood desks with comfy chairs, and pigeonholes with pouffes. Billy renamed it "Palazzo St Peter's" after his Glasgow kindergarten. As a final "fuck-you" gesture, it could not have been more apt.

A handsome, butter-coloured limestone called globigerina is used in most local construction. It is hewn and heaved from vast quarries that indent the main island in so many sites one wonders if eventually there'll be just one fathomless chasm, into which everything else will topple. The most durable limestone is excavated from the deepest quarry level, and it comprises the best quality stonemasonry façades, ornamental balconies, scroll-embellished porticoes and chubby balustrades. The buildings are uniform and graceful, except for a few, shocking, high-rise monstrosities, which blight some of the loveliest seascapes in the main tourist areas. The "What the hell were they thinking?" school of high-rise construction is alive and well in certain parts of Malta, where you can see architectural shockers that will take your breath away.

Our tiny, medieval street is a strip of small farms with townhouse frontages. Unless you live there, and rise early to scrub your front step with all the other homeowners, you might be forgiven for thinking there's no one else in residence. Maltese people hide from the sun, in deep, dark, grotto-like living rooms. Many dwell with animals: horses and pigs, and birds enclosed in rooftop aviaries. With so few trees in the place, I suppose even sparrows are prized. Our most vocal next-door neighbours are finches, pigeons and the occasional sow. Trap-ponies prance by in the early evening, in training for street-races, scrutinised by local punters in white vests, braces and crumpled hats. Some people even exercise their horses from moving cars, with sleepy kids holding the reins through the back window.

When Maltese people who've emigrated to Australia, Britain or the United States return back home, they rename their houses after the countries they abandoned: "America the Beautiful", "England Forever" or "Southern Cross". That is something Billy truly understands, for he speaks admiringly about many of the world's great countries and cities: Sydney, New York, San Francisco, Hong Kong, but his heart always returns him lovingly to Scotland. On the other hand, he merrily lampoons Scottish people who pine for the Old Country in song, even when they're at home.

"They're warbling about roaming far away and missing the purple-heathered hills of home, when they're sitting in their living room right in the middle of Partick," he scoffs.

The capital city of Valletta has many quirky features, not the least of which are "argument houses" as they're known: places where the occupant has died and the family quarrels about ownership remain unresolved. I'm glad we didn't buy one of those. Billy took me to see one that was rotting away down a side street near the citadel. As we peered through cracks in a flaking wooden door, we saw upholstered chairs bestrewn with thick grey dust, once-pale curtains now a filthy charcoal, and grime-laden men's suits still hanging in the wardrobe, from eighty years past.

There is so much that intrigues me about the place. I became enthralled with the history of the Knights of St John of Jerusalem, a bellicose order of crusaders who ruled Malta from 1530. They had a bizarre penchant for building gargantuan, baroque cathedrals right in the middle of farming land, but they fortified the harbour and resisted invading Turks. Between them, they even managed to give Nelson and Napoleon a run for their money. I bought some portraits of the sombre, bearded noblemen to hang in the entrance hall.

"Get rid of them," cried Billy furiously. "Miserable-looking fuckers."

Not long after we first arrived, Billy and I motored around the main island, enjoying the cheese-slice cliffs and Gatorade sea, red stone forts and donkey trails. One of the big advantages of Malta, for a sand-hater such as Billy, is that it has a pomskizillious coast but comparatively few beaches.

"I wish I had a boat," moaned Billy, for the millionth time.

"Why not get one?" I suggested, for the zillionth time. It was a never-ending saga. He wanted one, but then he didn't. Where would we keep it? What would it cost? Who would keep an eye on it? Could he learn to sail it? As we gazed across the placid stretch of water to Comino, the smallest of the Maltese islands, I wondered if he dared imagine all the fine, salty adventures he could have by its famous blue lagoon.

"You know, the America's Cup should be a full contact sport," he mused. "Repel all boarders. It's the only way you're going to make that bunch of stiffies interesting. Have them capture other boats and make the people walk the plank."

As afternoon fell, we lingered in towns with steep, cobbled lanes, browsed in hand-blown glassware shops and snickered at pantalooned sentry guards. When we paused to eat fresh octopus in a beach-side cafe we were close to a sloppily maintained film set, once built for the movie *Popeye* and now a tourist attraction. Breathing deeply, we surveyed the coast and the rock-ribbed hills.

"I had a night out here with Harry Nilsson once," began Billy, "when he was doing the music for *Popeye*." Harry was an American singer and songwriter, who brilliantly married sentiment and cynicism in several much-admired albums. My favourite among his lyrics was always his version of "It Had to Be You":

There's no one else, it's you I adore
When you stand up, your hands touch the floor.

"We were both legless that afternoon," continued Billy. "For a laugh, Harry had just charcoaled his name in colossal letters on a castle fort and he said if I in turn could write my name big enough to be seen from the film set, he'd make me a knight of the Maltese Cross."

76

Billy, of course, accepted the challenge. The two of them clambered up to a suitable boulder, and Billy wrote his name in scrawl as tall and broad as he could manage, given his state of inebriation and attendant loss of coordination.

"Right. Now make me a knight." Billy nearly lost his foothold while attempting to admire his Holy Grailaffiti. Harry pulled out a plastic lighter, decorated with a Maltese Cross, and presented it to Billy with a wobbly flourish.

"You are now one of us," he said grandly. "Have you any drugs?"

"What?" said Billy, "No!" At that point in his life Billy preferred to drink himself comatose, rather than alter his level of consciousness.

"What are you doing tonight?" asked Harry.

"I don't know." Billy was a little worried. He was there on business and thought perhaps he ought to look interested. Nah.

"Let's have another drink, then!" Harry decided. The pair charged off around the island, slurping more brandy and treasure-hunting for pharmaceuticals.

Harry was one of Billy's heroes. Here was a chance to tell him how much he liked his songs, and how he had tricked his father into listening to the one that goes:

> *You're breaking my heart*
> *You've torn it apart*
> *So fuck you!*

"It was a great laugh," he said, "watching my father's disbelief."

Billy's father was a stalwart Catholic, for whom profanity was pestilence and anarchy an abomination. Billy endured his lambasting until he was old enough to spot hypocrisy; thence-forward the torpedoing of his father's pseudo-saintliness became his subconscious life mission.

As the night wore on, Harry had an inspiration.

"Come," he ordered. "I'll show you this place."

They went to a gas station where some bored-looking people were sitting around waiting for a guitarist who never arrived. There was a piano in the corner that some vandal with a decorating bent had painted glossy green. Harry went over and tried the keys. It was vaguely in tune. He dragged a bar stool over to the piano and perched with his backside higher than the keys, and his arm drooping down.

"What'll I sing?" he asked.

"Remember Christmas!" It was Billy's favourite, and Harry performed it flawlessly for Billy and two men in overalls.

"It was one of the nicest wee musical moments in my entire life," says Billy. "Harry said he'd only ever done one live gig, 'I'm a Lumberjack' with the Pythons, but he was so pissed, he fell off the stage. I checked it out with Eric Idle, and it was the truth."

Our main problem in Malta is the tourist season. We want it all to ourselves.

"Oh it's you, Billy Connolly!" exclaimed a retired British woman in Rabat. "Well, I think you're awful funny, but I do wish you wouldn't swear."

"Well, watch someone else then," retorted Billy, good-naturedly. "Try Tom O'Connor . . . that'll be nice and safe."

Billy's daily walks are curtailed when tourists are about, which does no good to his waistline. Until recently he had little trouble staying in shape. He eats carefully if you don't count the occasional Indian curry blow-out. "I could murder a big Indian" he'll say from time to time, charging off to a takeaway restaurant that features indoor waterfalls and gold-embossed scenes of the Taj Mahal hung sparsely over red striped wallpaper. He'll order onion bhajis, vegetable samosas, and chicken bhuna with a pishwari naan. Then, in anticipation of "fiery bum syndrome", he'll sometimes phone home to ask me to put the toilet paper in the fridge.

When Billy's touring he loses weight at an alarming pace so it doesn't seem to matter if he gains a bit in between. With his sixtieth birthday approaching, however, he began for the first time in his life to worry about his weight. Coveting the tummy of a twenty-year-old, the "six-pack" or taut row of well-defined abs, Billy went on a mission of misinformed madness. Enthused by a series of hope-inspiring infomercials, he first bought the Abserciser, a contraption for minimising back pain during sit-ups that is still in its plastic wrapping.

Then one day I came home and found him reclining in front of the television, with an apparatus consisting of strange little wires and electrodes attached to his stomach, administering electric shocks that were supposed to exercise his tummy muscles. I couldn't believe it: Billy Connolly, savage provocateur, enjoying a cup of tea with a pinch of Slendertone.

"Bloody rip-offs," he pouted, when his spare tyre refused to deflate.

Malta is a Catholic country, and its art reflects that. I happen to like religious icons: the painted kind, with gold leaf and Russian inscriptions. I bought two or three contemporary ones for the house but, knowing that Billy, as a resentful ex-Catholic, would not appreciate them, especially the painted crucifix, I stuck them in the guest bedroom and hoped he wouldn't notice.

"God, Pamsy!"

I froze. The voice was emanating from that very room.

When I caught up with Billy, he was staring at my turquoise and gold-painted crucifix. Before I could find a satisfactory excuse he let out an approving whistle.

"Will you look at the six-pack on Him!"

You cannot escape Jesus in Malta. Each town has its own annual religious festival, a summer time "Festa" weekend, during which huge icons are carried through thronging, flag-filled streets, accompanied by choirs, brass bands, and Brits in shorts. The churches and cathedrals are illuminated with cheap, coloured fairy lights, and if you peek inside you'll see the biggest plastic chandeliers in the universe. The Maltese love firecrackers and pyrotechnics. They spend more money on fireworks per capita than any other people in the world, which is perfectly obvious if you arrive during Festa time. It is impossible to escape the thunderous bangs and whizzes that blast the neighbourhoods from dawn to dawn. We climbed on to the roof to watch the procession in our village. Yellow and white Vatican flags flapped from every rooftop.

"Those flags have a Versace look about them, don't you think?" said Billy, having learned about the Italian designer from Elton John. That was not Billy's only lateral supposition. "I guess they explode all those bombs in the air to exercise their racing pigeons."

As the procession advanced the grotesqueness of the scene became more apparent. The cheering, fervent throng surrounded acolytes in elaborate green and gold robes with tasselled belts, shouldering a twenty-foot statue of the Virgin Mary. It swayed alarmingly from side to side, swiping the flag-decked balconies on either side of the street.

"Will you look at that!" whistled Billy. "People are sticking money and jewellery on a doll!" It was a frenzy of Mary-pride. The bands were so close to each other there were moments when you could hear two cacophonous tunes at once, punctuated by the whirring and crashing of fireworks, the cheering and fervour of the throng. Billy really enjoys marching bands, flute bands and mariachi bands. He particularly likes their trousers and prefers them to have exotic names like Clive Palmer's Moyshe McStiff and the Tartan Lancers of the Sacred Heart.

"Bands are the only kinds of musical groups in the world that sound better out of tune," he says. "I like them when they're good and love them when they're bad."

"I think 'Goodnight, John Boy' would be a great name for a band, don't you?" shouted Billy above the din. "Or 'The Last Tank Top in Partick' or 'Big Jessie's Pinkie'."

Perhaps the bejewelled Virgin Mary heard Billy's prayer and intervened, for at the end of April a miracle occurred: Billy finally got his boat. A 19-foot open sailing boat called a Drascombe Lugger, a generous early birthday present from his manager Steve, turned up at the marina. To finally receive such a beautiful, longed-for prize filled him with ambivalence as well as gratefulness.

"It's absolutely gromphibberous." Just like Lear, he was beyond real words. Interestingly, he was also beyond action. Even though he knew it was sitting rigged and ready for him on the water, Billy could not bring himself to venture dockside for several days, since he struggled with the belief that it was really his. When he finally saw its gleaming black hull and pearly sail, it took his breath away. It was a glimmering, real-size version of the toy yacht his father had brought home from the war in 1943. For Billy nowadays, such boats symbolise unfettered giving, innocence and freedom, a hugely powerful combination.

"I think I'll call it *Wee Jessie*," he announced, studying the operation manual.

"I thought boats had to be female," I demurred. In Scotland, a Jessie is a derogatory name for an effeminate man.

"Exactly. Same difference. I heard about a catamaran called *Les Balles de Chien* or *The Dog's Bollocks*, but I agree boats should have female names. I think *Dolores* would be a great name for a boat, if only it didn't mean 'sorrow'." (Billy once wrote a song called "Dolores, Get Your Sweet Arse Over Here".)

Silence. Long moments of bewilderment, and frustrated sighing.

"Fuck. Listen to this," he read out loud from the manual.

"'Secure the throat gringle to the clevis pin in the jaws at the lower end of the gaff yard.'" I winced.

"There's worse. Read this . . ." I peered over his shoulder and read:

"'Insert the bumkin from aft.'"

"That sounds bad." He shook his head. "Probably something you'd get done for, if you tried it in the harbour. Nope, I won't be doing that till I'm way out at sea."

At the end of our first time in Malta, we had a "back to school" feeling as we took the 5a.m. helicopter flight to Valletta airport for a transfer to London. It was a dark and eerie journey. An ancient Russian war machine lifted off the ground with all the finesse of a sumo wrestler hauling himself out of an easy chair.

Billy's time in that peaceful, foreign place had calmed and soothed him. Like a solo-crossing sailor on a Western Isles windjammer, he had tempered his rageful ranting and volatile shtick; but I sensed he was eager to return to shore. His mounting anxiety about returning to America was becoming evident beneath his new irritation with all in sight.

"Don't put your make-up on in the dark, Pamsy. You'll end up looking like Bozo the Clown."

I gave him a "get out of my face" look.

"Could you show me how to do eye make-up? I think I'm going to start wearing eye-shadow."

Another look. This time, incredulity. I shook my head. It was always the same; whenever he's had a break, he comes bouncing back with a force I can barely handle.

"See them cats' eyes on the tarmac? They always remind me of McKenzie, the Australian flight attendant from Adelaide to Wyalla. Emu Airways it was called. When the aircraft was a thousand feet in the air, you suddenly realised that emus don't fly."

Slight smile, focus on lipstick.

"Anyway, McKenzie used to ask, why do they have cats' eyes on the runway?"

Raised eyebrows. It was a while since he'd told me a joke.

"'Cos if they used cats' arses, they'd need twice as many cats."

I tried not to wince, but I think he caught me. Billy was silent for only a minute or two before his *USA Today* newspaper yielded an extension of the theme, and brought him crashing back to his customary state of fury.

"Listen to this. Some tight-arsed prick is saying the US economy needs fiscal rectitude." He adopts an American accent. "*Fiscal rectitude?* Where the fuck did he come up with that one? I'd say it's the other way round. Compulsory *rectal fiscitude* for every politician is what it should be. That's how I'd run the place."

The Billy had landed.

CHAPTER
FIVE

"This Is An Accent, Not A Speech Impediment"

"It would be nice if they put a wee window in these things," thought Billy as the massive Beverley transporter teetered over the plains of Libya. The deafening hum and constant throbbing made it hard for him to be his usual chatty self. Otherwise this would be the perfect set-up for swapping a story or two: rows of bored men facing one another on skimpy hammock seats, all sandwiched into the metal hull of the ugly utilitarian war machine. Instead, Billy began to contemplate the task ahead.

"I hope I get down in one piece," he worried. "It'll be a bugger if I don't make it to my twenty-first birthday."

He thought of the factory workers who packed his parachute, and prayed they'd had their minds on the job. He nervously fingered the red tag on his breast that could open a reserve chute if necessary.

"Action Stations!"

Billy's adrenalin soared as the sergeant's words sent every man leaping to his feet, hooking his parachute to the overhead line and facing the door in readiness. As he'd done just twelve times before, Billy checked his own front buckles and the back of the similarly camouflaged man in front of him, then about-faced and checked those of his rear neighbour. Making a thirteenth jump might have been cause for concern for a non-military parachutist, but superstition and lucky charms were frowned upon in the Fifteenth Scottish Parachute Regiment.

As the exit door was wrenched open, Billy felt a blast of icy night air rush through the cabin.

"Fuck, it's dark out there," he thought, trying to breathe.

"Go! Go! Go! Go! Go!" shouted the sergeant. At each command another young man slid out into indigo clouds, until the sky was filled with people plummeting to the drop zone, a treeless field in Cyprus where their exercises would commence. Billy shuffled forward until he could feel his uniform flapping ferociously, then stuck one toe over the edge of the aircraft and one hand outside on the fuselage.

"Go!" It was his turn to launch himself off from the belly of the plane. White silk billowing behind him, he began his daunting descent. It was crowded up there. To his right he could hear men fighting. One had drifted below another, stealing his air and causing his parachute to start collapsing.

"Move, ya eejit!" yelled the frightened trooper, kicking furiously at the encroaching 'chute.

"Amazing," thought Billy, always able to take a lateral view. "He looks as if he's running across the top of it."

Billy pulled on one of his shoulder lines to guide his parachute out of the way of another fighting pair who had swung right into each other and were frantically trying to untangle themselves. They were dropping together at a faster rate than the others, cursing and punching as they went by. Billy licked his fingers and moistened his cheek so he could gauge the angle of his approach to the ground and prepare his body to roll when his feet hit the dirt.

Clunk! His weapon container landed a second before he did. He executed a perfect landing roll, and when he was upright again he quickly pulled his parachute in hand over hand and tied it in a little bundle. So far, so good. He listened in the darkness for a moment, then slung his Bren gun over his shoulder and took off as silently as he could in the direction of the greenish light that signalled their meeting place.

After half a mile or so, he began to climb a steep hill. His boots sensed a change of ground texture, and a strong scent of farm animals floated his way on the brisk breeze. Something didn't feel right. He could hear goats, pigs and chickens below him, and had a sense that he was standing on something hollow. He edged forward slightly, shoving one foot forward to feel ahead, until he realised he was just inches from a sudden drop. He strained harder to make out his surroundings.

"Jesus in heaven . . . I can't believe it," Billy whistled under his breath, realising that he was standing on top of a house with a roof that sloped all the way to the ground.

After Billy found his regiment and all were assembled, the men began to trek up into the leafy Kyrenia mountains, five abreast on either side of the road. Billy was glad he'd been given a Bren gun. Some men marched stealthily with rifles ready at the waist, but other poor bastards had to lug machine-guns. This exercise mission, to find a group of infantry called the Green Howards, might take a week or so and it would be uphill much of the way.

The task thoroughly suited Billy's sense of adventure, but it was hard. For five days of stealthy trekking they put up with horribly uncomfortable living: sleeping in ditches, eating rations, and assuming the bathroom habits of bears. Fortunately Billy had already learned to sleep anywhere, no matter how incommodious. He was even known to have a kip while on sentry duty.

"You sleeping, you?" his captain would bark.

"No, just resting my eyes."

"You bastard, Connolly. I'm watching you."

On the sixth day, when every man was thoroughly worn out, they finally captured the first Green Howards soldier from his hiding place in a tree-lined ridge. Hearing of this victory, Billy came walking up eagerly to where the "prisoner" was sitting on the ground, enjoying a cigarette.

"How ya doing?" said Billy, peering at him. The man looked at him a little sheepishly.

"Awright, Big Yin, yourself?" he said pleasantly. Billy immediately recognised him as an electrician who worked beside him in the shipyards.

"Fuck me, Tam," he said, a little deflated. "I didn't need to come all this way. I could have captured you last week in the canteen."

In May, Billy flew to Montreal to film *Timeline*, in which he was to play a time-travelling scientist. If Billy himself could have time-travelled back four hundred years from modern-day Montreal, he would have found himself in the native village of Hochelaga, discovered in the sixteenth century by the explorer Jacques Cartier, who was searching for a passage to India. The city has grown to be both culturally and architecturally diverse, with cobbled streets and skyscrapers housing people from pretty well everywhere. To this mix was added one more Scot, a wild-haired sleepy man stumbling off a jet in the dark and bitter early afternoon.

Billy stayed in the Quartier Latin area of Montreal, a place of bistros and boutiques, coffee shops and corner markets. The previous year I had attended a professional conference in Montreal, and had been billeted in a sterile, concrete convention establishment right in the centre of the business district that hosted cut-rate weddings, bar mitzvahs and high school reunions. By contrast, Billy's hotel had a pillow menu. When I called him he was choosing between goose down, duck down, hypoallergenic rubber, anti-snore neck roll and NASA space-pillow.

"I always prefer the mouse-down," he said.

Montreal boasts a biosphere, an exciting geometric dome designed by Buckminster Fuller that houses four distinct habitats: Amazonian rain forest, a marine ecosystem in a gigantic tank, a Laurentian forest with lynx, otters and beavers, and a polar world where penguins and puffins can be viewed. Billy saw none of it. Sometimes I think he should be the one to stay home, since I am probably constitutionally more suited to traipsing around the world, or at least I am more inclined to seeing points of interest when I do. In truth, the weather was particularly harsh, so Billy tended to stay indoors, choosing instead to adventure into literature and drawing.

It was unusual for Billy, allowing cold weather to dominate his behaviour. In the past, he has endorsed a rather Spartan attitude to harsh elements, but perhaps Californian life has raised his expectations. Denied the certainty of his regular walks, he bought a sketch book and art materials and set to work in his hotel room.

During summer holidays in Takapuna, New Zealand, when I was a child, my cousins and I would produce art we called "squiggle drawings". Each of us would take a blank piece of paper and scribble mindlessly on it with a pencil for half a minute, then swap the paper with someone else. We would then peer at that squiggle to elicit meaningful shapes, such as an eye or a tail that might eventually lead to a coloured painting of a huge fish. When Billy was a youngster, he and some fellow shipyard apprentices employed exactly the same drawing technique when they were slacking off work. They would make squiggles in chalk on the side of the ship, then stand back and try to decipher a form that would eventually take a more realistic shape.

Billy approached his new creative bent in exactly the same way. Using felt tip water pens, he produced most interesting coloured drawings and was surprised at how much pleasure it gave him. On finishing a piece he experienced a gratifying feeling of accomplishment that felt a bit like songwriting. Something appeared that hadn't existed before, through a birth that was always pleasing.

"Time passes at a phenomenal rate," he exclaimed when he first began. "You'd think one hour had elapsed but it would be four. I'd think, 'Well, that was a waste of time,' but then in the morning I'd go, 'Gosh, that's good.'"

Billy liked each drawing more than the last one, judging it fuller and more complicated, and he was really quite proud of the final images, with their jolly, stripy backgrounds. He named them *The Secret Life of Geometry* (red, yellow, black and white); *Meanwhile in the Long Grass* (browny-greeny worms with metallic flashes); and *Robert Burns and Mary of Argyle* (black-and-white checks and vivid greens and blues). My favourite is entitled *What Japanese Flags Do When You're Not Looking*, in red and white with a Munch-type screaming face.

When it wasn't too wet, Billy took a morning stroll. He likes to beat out a familiar path in every city he visits, and by his sixth day of exploration he had managed to establish a Montreal trail. It began to the right of the hotel where he found a couple of great book stores, one second-hand and one new. He pottered around in the former and picked up a lovely old complete set of the novels of Charles Dickens. When he reached the main street, he looked for a ranting homeless man with plastic bags on his feet who usually loitered in the doorway of an empty office building. Billy is drawn to tramps, half envying their lonesome nomadic lives. At some level he regards them as lucky escapees of a cruel bedlam, rather than the opposite. The man with the plastic bags on his feet took Billy's handout grudgingly as if he were doing him a favour and, recognising a fellow grouch, Billy liked him all the more.

Another homeless man, on the opposite corner of the busy intersection, seemed more appreciative of Billy's generosity. He grinned at passers-by, and played spoons to Irish music emanating from a tinny boom box. Billy began to jig a little, *Riverdance* style, with arms folded behind his back until he got too puffed and had to stop. "I should write a musical about drunk people and call it Liver Dance," he said, hoping for conversation, but the man just stared at him with a far off look, moistening his lips.

A store selling cigar accoutrements was a little further west on the left-hand side and Billy tried to pass it without purchasing a Montecristo. He has supposedly given up smoking them, but he still keeps his cigar-clipper and humidor handy for a relapse. In Los Angeles, Billy fully embraced the fast-growing cigar culture. He loves to sit with other men and shoot the breeze . . . except that to my way of thinking the only breeze around cigar-smokers is second-hand and carcinogenic. He enjoyed the pastime so much the children came to know the telephone number of the cigar store by heart, and it was then that I became a killjoy.

"Och, Pamela," he said, "nobody dies of death."

Since Canada has never severed diplomatic ties with Cuba, it is easy to buy Cuban cigars at any tobacconist in Montreal. Billy stared in at the assorted offerings and craved the aroma of the rolled, gold-brown leaves, all nestled together in colourfully decorated boxes. He would have loved the cigar factory I once visited in Cuba where smiling, dark-haired women hand-rolled the cigars on their bare thighs. He would also have enjoyed seeing Ernest Hemingway's house, a white, open-shuttered colonial dwelling with wide balconies and a swimming pool where Ava Gardner once swam nude. In a jealous pique, the story goes, Hemingway's wife humiliated the supposed object of her husband's desire by whipping away her clothing from beside the pool. Gardner was thus forced to dart up to the house stark naked, observed by the household, guests and staff alike. I knew that Hemingway had kept scores of pet animals, but none were anywhere to be seen.

"Where are all the cats?" I enquired. My guide shrugged his shoulders. "During the revolution," he explained, "there were many hungry Cubans."

A little further on from the cigar store was a large, bustling French cafe, which in sunny weather could be opened up to the street. Right now it was glassed off from the elements, and Billy could see people inside eating continental breakfasts. He peeked in and took a deep whiff of *fromage*, wine, and potent coffee. Billy sees himself as a hard-edge cafe society participant, a man who takes his *citron pressé* minus sugar, just like his porridge. Given a choice, he would always choose Cullen Skink (a wonderful Scottish smoked fish soup) over *soup à l'oignon*, but he is nevertheless partial to a baguette with a slice of cheese and tomato, and considers *tarte aux pommes* a culinary miracle.

He liked the cheery atmosphere of shouting waiters and banging plates. Billy utterly approves of the European style of talking, singing, eating and drinking all at the same time. He himself often attempts to multitask while he masticates, which is why Jimmy Tarbuck calls him a messy eater. "I need a slobber-garde," Billy says, pretending that it's a German invention.

The grocery store had to be avoided. Frankly, he would make a detour past any shop that sold Brussels sprouts, for as a child he was viciously beaten until he ate them. Billy jaywalked across the street to an ice-covered mailbox and continued on the other side of the thoroughfare to Ben and Jerry's ice-cream store, where he bought a small vanilla cone before doubling back to the hotel. All in all it was a good walk, of about one mile, trudging along in his silver cowboy moon boots.

There was endless night-shooting on *Timeline*. It was freezing, muddy and generally uncomfortable on that location, but Billy thought the end result was miraculous. A full-size, eleventh-century French chateau fort was constructed specially for the movie, way out in the Quebec countryside. It was so realistic, the first time Billy saw it he had to touch it with his hand to be convinced it was not made of stone. The production builders even erected an authentic-looking trebuchet, or giant sling shot, to hurl huge pots of burning oil at the castle for the battle scenes. He loved to slosh around outside when special effects were in progress, marvelling as fantastic fiery arrows streaked their way across the inky sky.

As an actor, Billy is fond of improvisation. The movie's director, Richard Donner (famous for movie hits such as *Lethal Weapon*), allowed Billy to be his inventive self and treat the script as a rough guide to the dialogue. At one point the actor Paul Walker, who played Billy's son, improvised an impersonation of his screen father's manner of speech.

"This is an accent, not a speech impediment!" Billy improvised back. "That's a take!" yelled Richard Donner.

"I love Billy," Donner said to me afterwards. "I've loved his comedy for ever, and I fell in love with him in *Mrs Brown*. He brought that character to life in such an understanding and sensitive way."

"What was he like working on your film?"

"What a handful!" He gave a throaty, appreciative chuckle. "You never know where he's going. It's like you're a passenger in his racecar and he's blindfolded."

Richard came to the conclusion that he had never understood the English language until it was interpreted by this particular Scotsman, and was arrested by Billy's linguistic style every time they spoke. Billy, meantime, was experiencing the English language in quite a different form, for when he wasn't working he was catching up on the novels of Charles Dickens.

"It's the nineteenth century in my dressing room, and alternately the eleventh and twenty-sixth centuries up at the gig!" he told me over the phone.

As a boy, Billy found solace and a welcome escape from his home life through Glasgow's excellent public library system. His foray into Dickens provided a similar respite, this time from the rigours of filming. He began with *The Old Curiosity Shop* and *Hard Times*, then moved on to *Oliver Twist* and *David Copperfield*. Billy loved Dickens's dynamic, descriptive style, and the fact that all his sense were always thoroughly engaged. "With Dickens, you can almost *smell* it," he said.

Billy felt a bond with the characters through the austerity of their early lives, but most importantly, in the writer himself, he recognised a fellow piecemeal artist. Billy's comedic artistry is a conglomeration of bits and pieces that sneak into his brain, are skinned, squeezed, whisked and boiled, and emerge as a brilliant comedy dinner . . . only he does not start at soup and end at pudding.

Billy was elated to discover that Charles Dickens operated in a similar fashion. He had not set out to write novels but, rather, wrote serial episodes for monthly or weekly publications. Billy felt a sense of connection with Dickens's original readership, people waiting impatiently by news-stands for the next instalment. It reminded him of his own childhood, when he simply couldn't wait to find out what Flash Gordon did next. Dickens's egalitarian sensibility also endeared him to Billy, who recognised his love for the working class.

"He wasn't one of them but he found them very interesting and he was right," said Billy. "Before him, people wrote off the working class as uninteresting and dispensable. I'll always remember *Timeline* because of Dickens."

It was lovely to see Billy's newly fired literary passion. In the throes of delighting in Dickensian language, he was always eager to share revelations about the origins of expressions like "brand new".

"In those days," he told the girls over a speaker phone, "when they transported china and tableware, they were packed in bran, as in *bran new*, without the '*d*'. A sign of being new was flecks of bran on cups and plates. It was their equivalent of bubble wrap."

"Wow," they chorused.

"And do you know where 'hobnob' comes from? Then it meant clinking glasses together. There was a song at the time with the words 'hob and nob the musical glasses'. I love when I learn stuff like that."

I swear he's a closet linguist. He is particularly proud of words that come from Scottish dialects, and it's a treat to hear him use lovely words like *glakit* (stupid), *blether* (incessant chatter) and *crabbit* (grumpy). Billy really does use them in a completely natural way. Even if they are foreign to me they tend to be onomatopoeic so I can usually guess their meaning.

"Och, stop your foutering," he'll say to me if I'm fiddling incompetently with something or other.

"He's dead gallus," he'll say about a stylish friend, meaning he's confident or impressive to the point of cheekiness. Gallus came from the word "gallows" since the word originally meant "deserving to be hanged".

After he'd read four or five Dickens novels, Billy began to moan to me, during our telephone conversations, that he wished he'd read Tolstoy and Dostoevsky.

"Some of these guys have been running round my head all my life saying, 'Read me! Read me!' Shakespeare, for instance, which I don't even like reading that much. I find it fucking difficult running for the dictionary all the time . . ." He was on a roll. "Burns too . . . although I must say they do have their moments. I never admit that to people 'cos they'd look at me like I'd just farted at their wedding."

I was probably wearing that same look when he said that.

"It's a bit like Kenneth Branagh," he finally said.

"Branagh?" This was difficult. In a telephone conversation with Billy one must fully concentrate, since at least one of us has to follow the drift. I'd been distracted by TV news images of Bin Laden.

"Aye, people go to see Branagh's films because they think it's good for them. I mean he's a great actor and everything and enjoyable to watch, but he's also the Brussels sprouts of show business."

"If he's the Brussels sprouts of show business," I asked, "then what are you?"

"Och, I'm more the type of fattening, cakey food," he said. "People come to see me *despite* the fact that they think I'm going to be bad for them, a sort of sinful pleasure. I'm the treacle pudding of show business."

It was in the parachute regiment that Billy first set eyes on a treacle pudding; in fact he has actually seen one levitate. Travelling back to Britain after the Cyprus exercises, Billy was allocated the worst seat in the plane, right in front of the flapping toilet door. He was bored, uncomfortable and hungry, so he decided to eat the remainder of his twenty-four-hour rations. Each man had been given food supplies that included tins of Spam and a biscuit that could either be eaten dry, or moistened into a porridge. Best of all was the daily tinned treacle pudding, and Billy still had one left. Balancing precariously on his jump seat, he took out his special army tin-opener-cum-spoon, opened up the container, and took a satisfying spoonful of sickly sweet, sticky sponge goo. He had barely swallowed it when there was an almighty crack from outside the aircraft. The troop carrier dropped like a stone. Billy's torso stayed in its seat, secured in place by the seatbelt, but his legs floated right up to his shoulders. Though frightened to death, Billy was distracted by an absolute miracle performed by the pudding. It shot out of the tin like a baby sputnik and floated weightlessly in the air until he put a hand out to catch it. Later they discovered that lightning had hit the wing and punctured an empty fuel tank. Terrifying as the moment of impact was, he thought the pudding-trick was brilliant.

100

The aircraft managed to land in Malta where Billy and the other men hung around aimlessly for a few days, killing time with card games and stories, and queuing up to be shaved by the local barber with a cut-throat razor. That was a first for Billy, since the instrument was more familiar to him as a weapon used by Glasgow hard men. They call a scar a second prize.

Despite Billy's assumption that his flyaway beard had won him the "mad scientist" part, the make-up department asked him to submit to a clean shave. I called him at his hotel in Montreal just after he had been scraped and smoothed.

"Oh hello!" He sounded slightly put out. "I'm just having a wee lunch with Anna Friel, who's in the movie too. We just went cycling into Vieux-Montreal."

"Oh, good." (Slight twinge of jealousy, well-concealed.) "I'm . . . glad you're getting out on your bike . . ."

Of late, Billy has cycled less and less. He used to flop sweatily into the house, all spandex shorts and garish, drip-dry, streamlined bike shirt, but now he glides to a halt in the kitchen with a faint scent of forbidden cigars. He has loved bikes and cycling since boyhood, and was a Tour de France fantasist from the moment he mounted his first shiny, burgundy racer. He thoroughly admires the fit, brave and bold master sportsmen who partake in the Tour de France, gods like Bernard Hinault who can fall into a ravine, break a collar bone, then get back on the bike and still win the yellow jersey.

"When you weigh people like him against all those big Jessies that pretend to be injured in football, the guy's a superman," says Billy.

Billy is always impressed by people who surmount incredible odds to achieve a victory or stay alive. Their stories resonate with his own experience of triumph over adversity. It has become apparent that Billy had an early understanding of the way in which great perseverance and suffering could have either of two outcomes: achievement or frustration. The tales told to children are interesting to me, some being a culture's way of teaching a model of behaviour, either through a didactic folktale or a story like *The Little Engine That Could*. Occasionally, the tales seem intended to prepare children for the inevitable frustrations associated with class barriers. In Glasgow, there was a working-class story in which effort is far from rewarded:

When Billy was a boy, there were rag and bone men who would travel the streets with horse and cart, rattling two plates together and calling "Delft for rags!" (Delftware was a sought-after brand of dinnerware). It was a pinched-face, pipe-smoking Donegal Irishman who collected people's unwanted goods in Billy's neighbourhood. He wore old country-style moleskin trousers tied at the knees with string called Nicky Tams, to stop the rats running up his legs. On this day he noticed a woman beckoning to him out of a window on the ninth floor.

"She must have something good," he said to himself. "I'd better go up."

After climbing a couple of floors he was tired of hauling all his stuff along with him, but he persevered. By the fifth floor he was exhausted, but he was persuaded to continue with the thought, "Och, you never know. She just might have brass candlesticks." By the seventh floor he was coughing up his lungs, but a voice inside him said, "You never know, she might have silver, maybe solid silver." On the eighth floor he was close to passing out.

"This better be worth it," he was now saying to himself, "but you never know, those candlesticks might even be solid gold." When he finally reached the top, he knocked on the door and a harried housewife opened it. She was empty-handed.

"Thank God ye're here," she said, pointing into the room to a cheeky-looking four-year-old who was playing on a floral carpet. "Tell him, will ye," she commanded, "if he's a bad boy ye'll take him away in yer cart?"

In Montreal, Billy's most frustrating challenge was being prevented from attending the Scottish Cup Final at Hampden Park because he was in the wrong country. Instead, the Montreal-Celtic Supporters Club kindly invited him to watch it on a big screen television. He drove out of the city to a shopping mall in the suburbs, where forty or so expatriate Scottish men were all gathered in an Italian restaurant. It was only ten in the morning, so Billy sat down with them to watch the game over a breakfast fry-up. Many were draped in Celtic scarves over their supporters club shirt that featured both maple and four-leaf-clover motifs. This

103

little pocket of die-hards even sang rousing choruses of "Hail, hail the Celts are here" and "Over and over, we will follow you" at half time. Like Billy, the men all spoke French (it sounds great with a Glaswegian accent) and were thankful that their Scottish education had taught them the basics of the language so they could be successful in that country.

When Billy began to study French at St Gerard's, one of his classmates was a boy called Jim Lavelle. Everyone had to practise saying "My name is . . ." in French, but when Jim stood up in front of the class and announced "Je m'appelle Jim Lavelle" the others collapsed at the silly-sounding rhyme and he became "Je m'a" from then on. Billy himself was tickled to be known as Guillaume, French for William. The Cup Final breakfast, however, turned out to be a sad occasion, since their team was roundly beaten by Rangers.

Billy holds to a precept that warns, *Never join anything or play any sport for which you must wear special clothes*, and he is acutely aware of class issues when it comes to any pastime. For Billy, it is football yes, tennis no. That always confuses me, because in Australia where I was raised, tennis is not a class game, for anyone can hit a ball round a dusty earth court.

The most class-ridden, and indeed frustrating sport Billy has ever played was elephant polo at the World Championships in Nepal; although, in fairness, he did not need special clothes beyond a team polo shirt. In fact, all his luggage was stolen in India on the way to Kathmandu for the match, including his much loved

Davy Crockett hat. Billy still entertains hopes of getting that back.

"I know how they'll find it," he assures himself. "There'll be some ridiculously hot bugger wearing it. That can't be difficult to spot in India."

I was pregnant at the time so Billy went to Nepal without me. I longed to accompany him. I wish I could have seen him in his chic maroon and gold Cartier team polo shirt that he had to wear with Hush Puppies (the only shoes he was left with after the robbers struck) sitting uncomfortably behind the mahout (elephant rider) and instructing him which way to turn the elephant. When Billy discovered that the class system was at work on the Nepalese polo field and that people were obsequious to the maharajahs and allowed them to win, he took a Glaswegian approach. "Sometimes the mahouts want to play their own game and you have to get quite violent," said Billy. "I had to tell mine, 'Right, you bastard. Never mind the maharajah, just go for it.'" In the end, Billy won an ashtray for coming in third last.

Billy was not drawn to the sensation-tourism on offer in the evenings in the Chitwan wildlife reserve, for watching a Bengal tiger jumping on a tethered buffalo calf was not his cup of tea. Instead, he went out after dinner to see if he could spot a tiger. Those gorgeous big stripy cats were once hunted to near extinction by kings and guests of the maharajas, but they have been able to survive to contemporary times because they have been protected within the Chitwan reserve. Billy set out into the moonlit forest hoping to see one, but

105

after he'd trekked a few miles in the tall grasslands of the floodplain, noisy with the squalling of macaque monkeys and surprised parrots, he began to have second thoughts. It didn't help when he was told that tigers hunt at night. Sniffing at the wind, his guide suddenly announced, "The tiger's getting closer. Can you smell it? It's like cat's piss."

"Eh, wait a minute," said Billy, pausing by a scarlet-flowered *kusum* sapling. "It's just dawned on me what I'm doing here. I'm actually tracking a tiger. What if it doesn't like the idea?"

He wondered if he might soon face considerable inconvenience, like having to run a mile in the dark, or perhaps climb a tree. Tigers, of course, can climb too.

"There's always the fuck-it factor," he decided, attempting to second-guess the tiger's powers of reasoning. It would be hard for the tiger to climb a tree while a human being was jabbing him in the eye with a stick. Billy just prayed it would think, "Fuck it, I'll try to sneak up on a fat tourist instead."

But wild beasts can strike anywhere, even on a westbound flight from Canada to California. On his way back to Los Angeles after the end of his filming stint in Montreal. Billy reclined thankfully in his seat. He stretched his legs and wriggled feet that were shod in Fred Astaire-type, two-tone brogues in black patent leather and black-and-white spotty leopard-print.

"I love your shoes," a woman said admiringly as she served him a cup of tea.

"Yeah," said Billy, bored and mischievous. "I got them in Mexico. This guy had a big box of Dalmatian pups so you could pick your own." It's the only time he's ever been smacked by a flight attendant.

Billy does believe one's physical contact with the planet should be stylish. He's got an eclectic collection of cowboy boots made of, as he says, weird things that were once quite happy swimming at the bottom of the sea, like sting-ray, eel and sea-bass. He once found salmon-skin shoes in Glasgow but didn't buy them, for the sales person was intolerant of his dithering. Billy sometimes panics in shops. He once tried on lilac brothel-creepers, suede lace-up shoes with a huge crepe sole, and strutted around the shop wondering if he should commit to the purchase. The sales assistant knew exactly how to play it. "They clash brilliantly with your lime green socks," he said, which closed the deal.

Billy admires interesting women's shoes, and he wishes I would wear more adventurous ones. To that end he has bought me quite a variety of attention-grabbing footwear: white leather shoes shaped like a hovercraft, purple velvet Doc Martens, and leather high-heels with five raised toe shapes at the front of each. I wore each of them at least once; however, most of the time business dressing precludes such outrageousness.

I once asked his opinion about some pointy-toed shoes I was considering purchasing to wear to work.

"They're OK," he turned up his nose, "but you should wear the crazies. I mean, those toes are very sharp, but there are other brilliant shapes in women's shoes."

"But these are professional shoes," I explained. "For work."

"They are?" he said. "What are you doing in there? Stabbing the eyes out of cockroaches?"

Billy's idea of fashion hell would be a belt that matched his footwear (especially a white one), so his is made of a turtle's belly. He wears a buckle with a real scorpion set in resin, but mourns the loss of his favourite: a skeleton in a monk's robe carrying a scythe, above the words "Syphilis, Killer of American Youth". In fact, Billy thinks neckties keep the trousers up every bit as well as a belt.

"He does wear a lot of unusual clothes for a heterosexual, and I'm using the word 'heterosexual' very loosely," says Robin Williams. "That's what drew me to him: the voice, the look, and clothes that even a drag queen would go 'Oh . . . please!'"

Billy's infatuation with interesting clothing has rubbed off on his children. When our middle daughter Amy heard there was a fire at Dolce & Gabana in Los Angeles she breathed in sharply and asked, "Are the clothes all OK?" Her father has taught all his children well, for they have become most adventurous style-seekers, each in an individual way. Walter, for example, was recently spotted wearing a sage green cardigan over a yellow-and-purple LA Lakers vest, a Royal Stewart tartan kilt, and black-and-yellow bumble-bee wellies with eyes and antennae. The worst thing anyone in the family could ever say about clothing in front of Billy is "a beige one would be very practical".

It's hard to rebel in our household. The closest Amy has come to that was finding a nicely behaved boyfriend with a good education.

"What, he's a Republican? Going into law?" Billy hit the roof.

When Billy finally made it home from Montreal at the end of May he faced a style crisis.

"Daddy, you'll never guess what!" said Scarlett at the dinner table. "My friends called me up and said, 'Your dad's in *USA News* wearing a green and black tiger print suit!'"

"Were his shoes shiny?" she'd replied, unfazed.

"I guess . . ." they'd shrugged.

"'Cos I polished them."

"What did it say underneath?" Billy asked, hoping for an approving nod from the fashion writers.

"'Tony the Tiger's Gay Uncle.'"

CHAPTER
SIX

"I Only Want To Go To Heaven If Hank Williams Is There"

"There's a rational explanation for everything," repeated Billy to himself as he lay shivering in his bed, waiting for the devil to come. At twenty years old he wished he could find a steady girlfriend to share his long nights of jumping out of his skin. There, in a rented room at his folkie friend Danny Kyle's house, he was always scared shitless at bedtime. Danny, who thought Billy's night terrors were nonsensical, was apt to play on them quite mercilessly. For example, he would attach a fishing line to Billy's blankets and surreptitiously tug at them so they moved around when he least expected it. Billy was convinced the place was haunted.

To make matters worse, earlier on this particular evening Billy had dared himself to see the movie *The Devil Rides Out*. Instead of helping him to master his fears as he'd hoped, he had returned home thoroughly spooked and found the house completely empty.

Feeling dead jumpy, he roamed around for a bit, finished off the last of a bottle of whisky, then sat tinkering on his banjo. At three in the morning he thought he'd better turn in. He lay there sleeplessly, continually rerunning frightening scenes from the movie in which a black, riderless horse charged relentlessly after ill-fated victims. After a while he repeated his mantra about rational explanations again and again until he at last began to slide into a calm repose.

Suddenly, his ears picked up something that sent his heart racing once more. He threw off the blankets so he could listen more intently. There it was. Dear Jesus, it really was! He began to quiver uncontrollably as he heard the unmistakable sound of a horse's hooves thundering up the street towards him.

"Get a grip," he whispered to himself, noticing he had instantly become drenched with perspiration. With a massive effort he dragged himself to the window and peered out. His jaw dropped, the blind snapped in his hand and he reeled back in utter panic. A large black riderless stallion was charging up and down the street outside his house, right there in the centre of Gallowhill.

"The devil's right outside! He's coming to get me!" Overcome with terror, Billy returned to his bed to make a last-ditch attempt to save himself by hiding beneath the blankets. Foetal-like, he covered his ears to drown the sound of his approaching doom.

It was a good move. The clip-clopping continued for a while, then disappeared downtown. Gradually, since no horned sprite came to fetch him, Billy began to relax. When Danny came home, he called out to tell him what he'd seen. His friend burst out laughing and phoned the constabulary.

"This might sound a wee bit silly," said Danny, "but my pal says there was a horse running around outside."

"Och, is that where that darned animal's got to?" they said. It had escaped from a nearby field.

"Bollocks," said Billy when he learned the truth. "I should have known the fucking thing was real. It did a pile of jobbies in the marigold patch."

The fear of the unknown is no longer an omnipresent factor in Billy's life. He welcomes the wee small hours (in fact he's quite nocturnal) and also embraces opportunities to venture where he has hitherto not been. Even though the thought that death, as the ultimate unknown destination, might be clip-clopping at his door some time within the next forty years does occasionally faze him, Billy has decided there could well be a positive side to being relegated to hell.

"I only want to go to heaven if Hank Williams is there," he's decided.

In any case, he has in recent years embraced a philosophy of life and death that tends to leave the devil out in the cold. His essentially Buddhist philosophical notions have helped to calm him, although he also expounds a number of unique notions on which he bestows labels such as *The Tea-Cup Theory*, in which he sees the universe as a cup sitting on the arm of a gigantic armchair. This and other uniquely Billyish hypotheses have been catalysts for his moving beyond the horrific and archaic images of mortal-sin punishments that were presented to him as a child in Catholic school, and that has been quite a relief.

Summer vacation for American schools is nearly three months long. The "lazy, hazy, crazy days of summer", as the song goes, give students a chance to play, catch up on sleep, attend summer camp, or travel. We had planned to take our two youngest teenage children to India in the second week of June, so they could help out at the Tickety-Boo Tea Houses, charity homes set up by Billy and his manager Steve some years ago for imperilled young girls rescued from the red-light district in Mumbai (once known as Bombay). But when Pakistan and India looked as if they might be launching missiles at each other, the Indian Embassy in Washington stopped issuing visas. In the meantime, however, we'd received every vaccination known to mankind, including rabies shots.

"Makes you want to look for a mad dog to give you a bite," Billy moaned. "We should all go to the zoo and stick an arm through the bars."

Later on, the permits came through, but by that time, things had changed. Billy injured his back while pretending to be a yoga instructor, and Amy was engaged in the final process of acquiring a California driver's permit, so it was just Scarlett and me who, as the advance guard, set off for southern India just as the humid, mosquito-rich monsoon season began.

"See you at the Taj Mahal!" waved Billy, the pain in his lower vertebrae causing him to lean perilously to one side.

"Get yourself straightened out!" We blew him a final kiss.

There must have been just six westerners on our London-Delhi 767 Airbus leg, which seemed a tad ominous.

"Do they know something we don't?" grimaced Scarlett, popping her malaria pill. She has inherited a healthy dose of her father's cynicism.

After a twenty-six-hour journey, our third change of aircraft came bouncing down to earth in Mumbai in an oven-hot early morning mist. The black and yellow Fiat taxis were buzzing bumble bees, waiting to ferry people to every part of this city of eight million inhabitants. As we approached its centre, we could see that people who lived in Mumbai each experienced life in very diverse ways. By a litter-strewn swamp on our left we saw a narrow shanty-town, inhabited by thousands of families who'd made their minuscule homes from the rubbish of the people who worked in the elegant contemporary steel-and-glass skyscraper towering on the right-hand side of the street. As we stopped at a traffic lights corner in a relatively well-to-do neighbourhood in the city's centre, we noticed a mother seated on the ground with her small family. She motioned to her youngest walking child, a boy of around three, to approach us. He was so small we could not see his head beside our vehicle, but the sight of his tiny brown fingers clawing at our window aroused in us the kind of horror that would become all too familiar over the next three weeks.

"White man's guilt" is a powerful emotion. Were the people who slept on the pavement below our hotel window aware they had chosen the very best place to arouse compassion, fury, disgust and helplessness in the well-heeled foreigners like ourselves who rested between crisp white linens by a marble bathroom? When we stood in the centre of our room we saw only the Indian Ocean sprawling out to meet a searing sky through the three windows of our enclosed balcony. A few paces to the right revealed the Gateway to India, a gloriously intricate filigreed and minaretted British Raj stone structure that was built especially to com-memorate the landing of King George V and Queen Mary in 1911. Three or four paces towards the window, however, provided a Seurat French pointillist impression, a kaleidoscope of vibrant dotted colours that, on closer inspection, were the saris of thronging fisherwomen from the Koli tribe, red-and-gold lined horse-drawn carriages, the shrubs and grasses of the adjacent park, and the darker rags worn by the hundreds of idle, jobless youths hanging about on the sea wall. An even closer inspection provided certain evidence of our close proximity to great misery.

The largest slum area in the whole of Asia was right there in Mumbai. The rubbish mounds and tin shacks are evident wherever you go. On our first evening we went down to the red-light district in one of the worst of these shanty towns to visit a night shelter supported by a charity called Jubilee Action where children, who

115

would otherwise be unsupervised while their mothers worked in the sex trade can be cared for. Oil lamps were just beginning to be lit in the narrow, squalid, overcrowded streets, lined with sinister huts made from bits of tin, wood and poly bags. A few open, one-seater barber's shops, unsavoury-looking food stalls and exposed roadside toilets were being patronised by prospective clients of numerous adjoining brothels. The working women stood in their doorways, usually in pairs or trios, adorned in pastel saris, floral hair accessories and silver nose jewellery. As they waited for their customers they chatted, giggled, argued with neighbours and ate fruit slices from passing tray-vendors. An orange-saried girl, with bare midriff and many toe-rings, scolded her small child whose insistent howling was interfering with a prospective sale. Children are supposed to hide under the bed and keep quiet, or fend for themselves on the streets. A grimy baby of nine months or so, with tiny gold anklets on each leg and soaked pantaloons, lay sleeping, and apparently unattended, on a wooden crate within inches of passing motorcycles.

The shelter was housed within a compound off one of the busiest brothel streets in the district. A contemporary Mother Teresa in a yellow sari, an ex-streetwalker herself, ran the place with a few committed volunteers. When their engaging welcome smiles disappeared for a second or two, there was a certain hollowness behind their eyes. The little girls had been told we were coming, and rose to their feet with fingers together in the traditional *namaste* greeting.

They were beautifully bathed and groomed, and each one in a party dress, peachy *kurta*, or even a western ensemble.

We wanted to know the age of the youngest child in the place and were brought a sad and clingy one-and-a-half-year-old from another room, with sticky-out ears and in a little green dress.

"She's not feeling herself," explained a volunteer in a matter-of-fact, apologetic tone. "Her mother just died from AIDS."

The children performed an action song for us, a loud and joyful show in Hindi. They were mainly girls.

"Where do little boys go?" I asked, but no one seemed to know. Later I heard they hung around the brothels, and were commandeered to run errands such as fetching cigarettes for customers.

"When do the children here go home?" asked Scarlett, but it seemed that, being obstacles to business, most of them were unwanted and simply stayed in the shelter.

The following day we went to the countryside to visit the Tickety-Boo Tea Houses, two buildings built and maintained by Billy's charity, where rescued girls who are thought to be particularly at risk are taken so they can be permanently housed, fed, clothed and schooled.

"Would it be obnoxious if I wore my new necklace?" asked Scarlett.

"Yes," I replied, pleased that she had thought of it. I knew she was struggling with this very sudden lesson in life-in-the-raw, but so were we all. But it was surely the

117

perfect antidote to the materialistic sensibilities of our society, and no bad thing.

A ten-year-old girl had been rescued from the Victoria Terminus train station the previous week. Her parents, both people who lack the powers of speech and hearing, are beggars who live on the streets. They had sold her to an elderly man for a week for five hundred rupees, but her cries had attracted the attention of one of the Tickety-Boo workers who took her to the safety of one of the Tea Houses. The newcomer came to meet us, all smiles and sea-green sari.

"What's it like here?" asked Scarlett, but the girl didn't answer.

"She's quite clean now, for I gave her a bath myself." A tired-looking woman who worked in the night shelter seemed keen to assure us we could shake her hand with impunity.

I glanced at Scarlett, knowing I would have to do a good deal of debriefing after all of this. It was a far cry from life in the elite Los Angeles enclave she inhabited. We climbed up and down the stairs from dormitory to dormitory. Charming girls brought us flowers, drawings, tea and flowery tablecloths they had embroidered themselves. They performed some traditional dances for us with grace and giggles, and answered our questions.

"Where are their fathers?" I wanted to know, but that too brought an awkward silence.

"Do they ever see their fathers?" I persisted, well out of earshot of the girls.

"Well, no one really knows who their fathers are," replied Dan, the British charity worker whose vision had helped Billy and Steve create the houses. "There are sometimes men around semi-permanently, but they could be pimps or part-time partners. We don't let them come anywhere near the houses."

The girls' mothers did not come to visit either. If they wanted to see the girls they had to meet them in a park under strict supervision. All of the girls were considered to be at great risk of being snatched back and returned to the brothels to earn money for their families through prostitution. Such a life would fall to them from the age of ten or so if they were not protected by the work of Tickety-Boo.

"What would you like to do after you finish school?" I asked one girl who was nervously awaiting the results of her final exams.

"Become a doctor," she replied with a beautiful, intelligent smile.

Two tiny brown hands sought mine. A three-year-old and a six-year-old, both dressed alike in yellow skirts and red tops, with their hair swept into perky bunches on the top of their heads, followed me around for the entire visit.

Danny pointed to the six-year-old, who had been so badly undernourished in her first few months of life she was still very small for her age. "I came across her when she was a baby just as she was about to be sold to a brothel for ten thousand rupees, about a hundred pounds. Because of Billy and the people in Britain who

119

buy Tickety-Boo tea, she has a place to be brought up and cared for."

I began to fantasise about adopting her, and the desire was strong. Could I do such a thing in my fifties? Would it be good for her? Would it be fair on our other children?

I called Billy that night, filled with feelings of compassion, righteous fury and motherly desire.

"How would you feel," I ventured, "about adopting one of these little ones?" I was amazed at his immediate willingness.

"Sure," said Billy. "We could do that."

"What do you think, Scarlett?" I consulted our youngest. Although she is compassionate, I saw from her face it would be hard for her.

"For now, let's just try to raise lots of money for Tickety-Boo to keep the houses going," I said, knowing it was a decision on which we would have to spend much time and thought. "The girls are so well cared for here, and they're within their own culture." The trouble was, the houses were already so full there was a desperate need for more. In fact, the existing structures had been designed to house half the number of girls who now lived there, and soon the organisers would be forced to turn away prospective newcomers.

The delay in receiving our visas meant that we missed the wedding of a girl from the Tickety-Boo Tea Houses. Asha, the first from the whole group to be married, had been brought to the houses five years ago when she was twelve. Her mother had died two years previously and she had taken care of her younger

120

brother and sister by begging on the streets and relying on the sporadic help of sex workers who had known her mother. It was considered an extraordinary triumph that this girl eventually found a husband. Indian society is such that a girl with Asha's background would not be accepted into most families if they knew about her past. Billy had brought her photo on stage six years ago during one of his London concerts that raised money for the Tea Houses.

"Look at this lovely wee girl," he showed the audience. "She's the reason I'm doing this."

"She's a married lady now," I reported. "Her husband seems very nice. Works with abandoned boys."

"Tell him I've got a bone to pick with him . . ." said Billy. "He didn't ask my permission to marry my wee Asha."

Billy says he spent much of his youth trying to be the country singer Hank Williams. Then he changed and tried to be Bob Dylan.

"There was a brief period," he said, "when I thought I'd like to be Loretta Lynn, but thankfully that didn't last long."

Some people, however, have a far less transitory desire to be of a different gender than the one that was assigned to them at birth. My professional mission in India was to try to meet members of the Hijra cult and carry out some research. Hijra are biologically male people who feel they are more like women and prefer female self-expression. They are known as eunuchs, because many of them have been castrated. I met my first interviewee in a down-market hotel, for Hijra are very marginalised in Indian culture and few establishments will allow them to enter. She arrived in a yellow female *kurta*, beautifully coiffed and made up, and all decked out with a great deal of gold jewellery. She promptly changed into a red sari with gold thread and became a thorough diva, until I began to ask her questions about her childhood which made her extremely sad.

She had been taken to live with Hijra at the age of five, when her parents could no longer bear the shame of having a boy in the family who felt he was a girl. The Hijra community thence became her family and she was raised by them. Being a guru now, she has her own followers. Whenever there is a birth, death, wedding or some other important occasion, they turn up at the household to provide a lucky blessing along with singing, dancing and the solicitation of funds. In accordance with tradition, I presented her with a sari and coconut to show that I accepted her as a woman. She in turn blessed my venture in India, honoured me with her story, and allowed her disciples to speak to me. In the process I gleaned a picture of severely traumatised people. They gained my respect for their ability to survive against such huge obstacles as illiteracy, total rejection by society, severe poverty and loss of the respected status they (as a group) once enjoyed.

Most of the people I subsequently interviewed had had their genitals entirely removed. In some cases the operation had been performed in a shockingly barbaric

122

fashion, either by midwives who treated the resultant wounds with hot oil and turmeric powder that was supposed to heal and prevent infection, or by doctors whose level of aftercare was not substantially better. Not surprisingly, the mortality rate was high — in fact I heard of nine recent deaths from the procedure. Those who survived the loss of their genitalia thereafter enjoyed a higher cult status, due to their perceived level of commitment. Other benefits included the reduction of facial and body hair, and the acquisition of an unsightly genital-site that can be used as a weapon; for castrated Hijra who are made unwelcome when they turn up at households to negotiate payment in exchange for their blessing of births or marriages lift their saris in order to scare and repulse the family.

I suppose it is not surprising that Billy had problems hearing about all this. Although I did not tell him too much about the interview process, he winced every time I used the word "castration". He stopped me mid-flow when I was giving him a detailed report of an interview I'd just had with a midwife.

"Fuck, Pamela," he complained, "could you spare me the gory details? I'm already throwing up my lunch."

In fact, that was literally true for Scarlett and me. Even though we'd been extremely careful about what we ate and drank, we'd become ill with some kind of dysentery right away. A headline in the daily Indian newspaper told the broader story: *Food Safety: A Distant Dream*. A few days, and several doses of Imodium later, we flew to New Delhi to begin a brief

123

sightseeing tour. By contrast with Mumbai, Delhi was a model city of wide streets, well-defended embassies, and British Raj-style hotels. One thing it had in common with all parts of India, however, was the driving.

"In Britain you drive on the left, and in America you drive on the right," smiled our guide, bobbing his head from side to side. "In India, it's optional."

The streets throughout the nation are truly chaotic. One rarely sees a bicycle or motorcycle carrying just one person; each is far more likely to be ferrying three or four. Women sit side-saddle with their shopping and a child or two on their knees.

I emailed Billy some pictures of these extraordinary street scenes. One showed a motorbike passenger with a billowing pink and gold sari zooming along behind a bus.

"I can't believe it," cried Billy after he downloaded the first batch. "She looks like she's about to paraglide!" Of late he has become far more computer-literate. The reward of being able to receive the Celtic scores at any time or place around the globe provided a strong impetus.

As Scarlett and I negotiated the streets, taxis honked to try to pass us, even when approaching a hill. They in turn were challenged by brightly painted buses with beads swinging across the windscreen, ploughing ahead wherever there was a potential space. On top of all that, it is quite common to see a white cow happily trotting along in the middle of it all.

"As for that brave bastard . . ." said Billy, referring to a photo I took of a man with a striped rickshaw taking on an enormous yellow truck carrying flammable chemicals by veering into its path with apparent nonchalance. My husband is always a sucker for the underdog.

"Crazy, more like," I interrupted him. "You would not have used the word 'brave' if you'd been there." Those of us who were white-knuckled our way through every journey.

As a safer option, we flew to Varanasi. The airport bore a sign declaring "The Holy City Welcomes You", but when I tried to photograph it a man in a camouflage uniform threatened me with his rifle. The twenty-eighth incarnation of the Lord Buddha is thought to have been here. Some of his remains are said to lie in the Sarnath temple, a one-roomed hall with murals of scenes from the Buddha's life and a tree under which he apparently gained enlightenment. As we toured the city, we flashed past citrus fruit stalls attended by bored men holding umbrellas, beautifully decorated women drawing water from an aluminium public pump, and old men in turbans crouching on the ground for an animated discussion. Eventually we reached a once-fashionable hotel room that was now thick with dust and locusts. I had to lift each one of the latter carefully outside with a tissue before Scarlett would go to bed.

The next day we rose at four in the morning to take a dawn ride in a rowing boat along the Ganges, its banks lined with *ghats*. All Hindus are expected to visit this site at least once in their lives for spiritual purification, so even at that hour it was packed with bathers. Some were local people, swimming across the river for exercise, but most had come for devotional reasons. Orange-robed holy men mingled with fervent pilgrims who had travelled here from every part of India. As the filmy orange sun rose above the deserted sandy banks on the other side of the river, they waded into the water right up to their necks, washing, chanting, and saying their prayers. Some fully immersed themselves, while some just sprinkled the holy water over their heads.

It was a difficult sight for us, as western, non-Hindus, to understand. For me it was unthinkable to dip even a little finger into water that was so obviously quite putrid.

"When a Hindu is dying, someone will put a few drops of the Ganges into his mouth," said our guide.

"Well, that should hasten the journey," I muttered to myself.

Ashok, our guide for the day, was a tall man with an engaging smile who was clad in a knee-length, white *kurta*. I suspected he was hoping we would consider him to be something of a spiritual guru and quite far along the Noble Eightfold Path (he was a Buddhist); however, there was an inch of grey regrowth at the roots of his dyed black hair, his beatific smile seemed cultivated, and he made the cardinal mistake of assuming we were all Christians who knew nothing about other philosophies. I remained silent and sullen for most of our journey; however, Scarlett chatted away, oblivious to the tension between me and our troop leader.

As we made our way to our rowing boat, pitifully thin begging arms held out tin bowls towards us and a teenager with leprosy thrust his stumps across our path. The Brahmins sat fat and regal beneath tattered umbrellas, waiting for lower-caste bathers to approach them to receive a *tikka*, or forehead mark of honour made from vermilion powder, in exchange for some rupees. We could easily identify the Shiva worshippers who had received ochre sandalwood horizontal stripes, but others had red or orange smudges, or the vertical stripes of Vishnu followers. Thrilling morning *ragas*, heavenly bells, and devotional singing and chanting emanated from an upper wooden balcony, where followers placed gifts of light, small candles at a shrine, before taking to the water. Ensconced beside our casting-off point, members of a Southern Indian family, recognisable by their darker skin and the vibrant temple saris (silk with zigzag borders) worn by the women, were lighting a small incense boat made from leaves and flowers, and floating it out with chanting and prayers.

We began to drift downstream. People were still sleeping atop painted boats moored together in a line. There was a dead cow decomposing in the water right beside a crowd of bathers.

"The cows are holy too." Ashok caught our horrified glances. "So once they die it is fitting that they should just get pushed into the river."

A little further down we passed a bankside crematorium, little more than an open fire with a viewing platform above it. Mourners with shaven heads poked at the remains of their loved ones, observed from above by a party of fair-haired tourists in shorts. In accordance with tradition, deceased people are brought here covered in new cloth, red for women and gold for men. When we first arrived in Varanasi we saw a gold-covered corpse on its way to the river, tied to the roof-rack of someone's jeep.

"People under twelve, and lepers too, are not cremated." Ashok was anxious to provide every detail of this Indian Way of Death. "They are simply weighted down with rocks and thrown into the river."

"Why's that?" Amazingly, Scarlett was still able to ask a question. I, on the other hand, was acutely dumbfounded.

"Until a person becomes twelve," he replied, "he has not achieved all sixteen of the Hindu sacramental stages. Therefore he cannot receive full cremation rights."

There was an elderly human head floating quite near us. I hoped Scarlett would not see it.

"Sometimes people throw half-burned adults into the river, but that causes pollution." Our guide bobbed his head in disapproval. We were about to pass an open sewer pipe. In my mind, I could just hear Billy's reaction. "Pollution? There's fucking wee jobbies, cow parts and lepers all swirling around in there. I doubt that someone's partly fried granny's going to make that much difference." It was the one time I was glad he wasn't there.

Nothing was making any sense. Here in this extraordinarily complex place where spirituality means everything and materialism is denigrated, the human form of both the living and the dead are ostensibly afforded so little respect we really had to catch our breath to take it all in. Profoundly shocked, we spent the rest of the day attempting to focus on the spirituality, the devotional aspect of Indian society that was evident everywhere in the country, but especially there by the Ganges.

We visited another Shiva temple where I was delighted to meet a swami who could explain the meaning of tantra to me. Having a strong interest in sexology, I was familiar with the western tantric practices that focused on sexual rituals, yet I had always had a hunch it had been bastardised from the original meaning. In fact the use of sexuality to awaken what Hindus call *kundalini* energy is only one of a number of ways to attain the highest level of spiritual awareness. Certain sects focus on sexuality as the main means, but most stress the importance of balance, and teach that meditation and charitable work, for example, are also important methods of reaching that higher spiritual plane.

Amy met us in Delhi later that day. When I greeted her she was wearing a pair of orange and purple round fish sunglasses.

"What else did you pack?" I asked indelicately.

She opened her bag and extracted four lollipops, a bubble-blowing contraption, a Green Cross Man comic, a Tribe Called Quest CD, a stack of Polaroid photos of her friends and a few tank tops.

"Did you bring any shirts with sleeves at all?" I enquired. This was not a country where women show their arms.

"No," she replied. "And I need a toothbrush."

"You should have seen what we saw this morning," said Scarlett. "People being burned in big fires."

Amy's eyes widened. She was quite impressed.

"Alive?" she gasped.

Amy is delightfully dotty. Sometimes she IS Marilyn Monroe in *Some Like It Hot* only much prettier.

"I've been learning some Hindi," she announced, consulting her book. "Listen: *Dard haha ho raba hai? Kya masik ho raha hai?*"

"What does that mean?" asked Scarlett.

"You seem to be in pain. Are you menstruating?"

"Try it on that policeman," suggested Scarlett.

Indian trains are wonderful things, and a wonderful respite from the chancy game of chicken one encounters every single moment on Indian roadways. There had also been three major train wrecks in India during the previous two months, but what the hell. We gaily chug-chugged down to Jhansi sipping tea and eating Kit-Kats plundered from the minibar in Delhi. We thundered past the red-rock ravines near Gwalior where Phoolan Devi, known as "the bandit queen", had led her desperate gang in pillaging raids on local towns.

130

Phoolan was quite a gal. Being of a lower caste, *shudra*, she had previously been gang-raped by fourteen men who thought it was their right as upper-caste *thakur* to do so. She survived to have her revenge, becoming the leader of an Indian-style "Robin Hood" gang who plundered the homes of the *thakur* people whom she felt had wronged her. She eventually identified all her alleged perpetrators, lined them up and shot them dead. Her notoriety turned to popularity in the Uttar Pradesh region, so in 1996 she won an election to become a member of parliament where she apparently conducted her political career in an idiosyncratic fashion until she was murdered in 2001.

There is a strong tradition of powerful women in India. We saw many statues of Lakshmi Bai, once Queen of the province of Jhansi, a remarkably valiant woman who, in 1858, led her own fourteen-thousand-strong rebel army on horseback in order to protect her kingdom from being annexed by the British Government. She is often depicted on a white charger with a sword in her hand and a baby on her back. Mothers are revered in India, a fact I felt moved to mention a number of times to my daughters whenever I felt the need for a little puissance.

Our four-hour train ride was, unfortunately, just half of our journey to our next destination of Khajuraho, site of the extraordinary Chandella temples. We travelled the rest of the roof-bouncing way by rut-ridden roads through parched countryside and dusty townships, until we arrived in Khajuraho with just enough light left to view several of the eleven miracles of sculpture and architecture that awaited us. One of the first panels we saw was a beautiful sculpted frieze of Vishnu holding a conch shell, symbolising the inner voice, and a wheel signifying the movement of life, straddling a Garuda, or eagle-like creature. Nearby was a hopeful sign, a twentieth-century temple structure that contained elements of three different points of view: a Hindu cupola, a Buddhist pagoda and a Muslim mosque. One of the most impressive things about India is that one billion diverse people somehow manage to live together at all.

Some of the Chandella temples are known for their beautifully carved erotic sculptures. I was dying to share them with Billy so I emailed some of them from an Internet cafe.

"Will you look at that guy!" whistled Billy. For a man who has talked endlessly on stage about "sheep-shagging" he seemed inordinately shocked at the depiction of an army commander pausing mid-battle to copulate with his horse. He was very taken with the multiple-partner sex scenes, and reminded me of one of our British dinner guests, who had brought all conversation to a halt with the loud and weary pronouncement: "Oh, I HATE orgies!" Every head turned towards this man for his following line: ". . . holding your stomach in for hours on end . . ."

I received an entirely different notion of tantra from our guide there in Khajuraho. He explained to me that some Hindu sects believe one can focus just on *makara*, or manner of attaining freedom from the cycle of birth and death, and that for some people who

132

worshipped in this place it was largely sexuality that was used to awaken the *kundalini* energy that would lead them to nirvana. This sect practised an early version of "swinging" called *Choli Margi*, or way of the sari-blouse, that was apparently quite prevalent in the Chandella period. The *cholis* (sari-blouses) of a group of women were put in a pot, which were subsequently drawn out by the same number of men. Each would then enjoy a brief sexual liaison with the owner. In Orange County, California, I informed our guide, they now do the same thing with car keys.

In those days, women were classified into four different types: *Padamini*, or rounded with lotus-petal shaped lips; *Kamini*, or very passionate; *Sankhani*, or well built with big breasts; and *Hasthini*, with athletic bodies.

"Which one do you think I am?" I asked Billy, who wisely didn't reply. It was comforting to be reminded of the changing fashions of beauty though the ages. The tenth-century Lakshmana temple showed women all with a full-figured aspect of beauty, while in the later, eleventh-century Kandariyea temple the women were depicted as less buxom, with slimmer torsos and legs.

"Nothing is new," smiled our guide, showing us what he called the "Monica Lewinsky" panel where a couple was having sex in a private office. In another one, a man and woman were dancing together exactly as if they were doing a modern boogie-woogie. He pointed out a statue of a man in a most athletic Kama Sutra pose who had broken legs.

"Don't try this at home," he said pointedly.

133

One group of people was busy making an aphrodisiac in a large pot, adding semen as necessary.

"It's amazing, Billy," I reported. "It was concrete evidence that even in those early societies where people were not so hung up about sex as they are now, some people seemed to need a little boost."

"Pamsy, you'd better not tell the Viagra people about that wee secret ingredient," laughed Billy, "or they'll all be interfering with themselves down at the Pfizer lab."

There was such movement and variety in the sculptures, as well as a sense that the depicted people were, in many ways, contemporary. In one panel a lady was soulfully writing a letter, while in another a woman in a short, transparent sari was checking out the love bites on her shoulder.

"It is written in the Kama Sutra that a woman has one hundred and fifty erogenous zones," announced our guide. "During love-making a man should not forget to touch or play with all of them. It is a technique to prolong love. But he should not touch them for too long or it might get tickly."

"Myself, I find the hundred and forty-ninth causes the most problems," sighed Billy. "Especially since my back's getting worse." He had decided to travel to Glasgow to receive treatment there from a familiar osteopath.

"Are you serious?" I was worried. "Well, we could always have phone sex."

I read aloud to him from the Kama Sutra aphorisms on love, particularly the section called "The Life of a Citizen".

" 'Near the couch, on the ground, should be a pot for spitting'," I read. "What a turn-on."

"Really?" said Billy. "I shall attend to that forthwith."

" 'After breakfast'," I continued, " 'parrots and other birds should be taught to speak, and the fighting of cocks, quails and rams should follow'."

"I'm obviously leading the wrong kind of life," said Billy glumly. "I'd better get with the programme."

The next day we were to take another train, this time to Agra, the home of the famous Taj Mahal. On our way to the railway station we had our first real experience of monsoon down-pouring, with cows, monkeys and people all sheltering close to trees or wading unprotected in the plains. We arrived too early at the platform, and were shadowed by con-artists, cased by pick-pockets and barraged by beggars. The latter were mostly children, who held out their metal bowls or small cupped hands with practised pleading expressions. Our guide had no patience with them. *"Chale! Chale!"* He tried to move them on without success.

After sunset we arrived in Agra, a city that came into its own in the sixteenth century when it became a Mughal capital. Waking next day to the view of the gorgeous Taj Mahal from our window was the kind of experience that made us wonder if we were either still dreaming, or in some Glaswegian curry restaurant with a trompe l'oeil wall. The history of the Taj's construction must surely be one of the greatest love stories ever known. Shah Jahan built the mausoleum for his beloved Persian wife Mumtaz Muhal, who died giving birth to their fourteenth child. She had been his devoted companion in both peace and war, and he spent most of his heartbroken widowerhood creating a palace fit for her remains to lie in.

Most people can conjure up a mental image of the Taj Mahal as an astoundingly beautiful, symmetrical white marble building that combines elements of Islamic architecture and Hindu decoration. However, to walk towards it down the central walkway, flanked by gardens mown by white bulls pulling a rusty, iron grass cutter, and observe its structural and artistic dimensions both deceive and captivate one's eye is a truly awe-inspiring experience. Just when you think you have a sense of its height you walk a few steps closer and it seems to tower more loftily, rather than the opposite as you might have expected. A close-up inspection is no less impressive; the delicate inlay work throughout the interior depicts mainly flowers (since religious symbols such as birds were not allowed). Finely drawn lotuses of flame-coloured cornelian from Yemen are flanked by shaded leaves of agate striped with fine black onyx from Iran, as well as irises and other European flowers formed with lapis lazuli from Sri Lanka, Chinese crystal, and turquoise from Tibet.

It took Shah Jahan twenty years to complete the task of honouring his Empress, whom he had loved sublimely and named The Chosen One of the Palace. For the last eight years of his life, however, he had little access to his magnificent labour of love, for he was imprisoned by his third son, Aurangzeb, in a bloody bid for the throne. Blighted with cataracts, Shah Jahan could still just about see the outline of the Taj from his prison tower in the rose-coloured sandstone citadel known as the Red Fort. When he was confined to bed he used a mirror to help him glimpse it merely by reflection.

I longed to have Billy with me, to hold his hand as we strolled in this most romantic place. In fact, we probably would have refrained from touching because public displays of affection are utterly frowned upon in India. Interestingly, the only people we saw holding hands that day were two young men; however, that did not mean the same thing it would have in West Hollywood. Jasmir, a gay man I met in Mumbai, told me that the gay community is very hidden in India, and that homosexuality is illegal.

"But then," he explained, "according to an arcane law, so is kite-flying."

It is upsetting to me that in many countries people are punished for their sexuality or rejected for having a gender identity that is at odds with their physical body. I heard such dreadful tales from the Hijra, Shivshaktis (temple prostitutes) and others I'd met in India, of abuse, ill-treatment and rejection, yet as always with such people, their resilience profoundly moved me.

The cultural differences between Indian people and our family seemed to be appreciated by all. Our fellow visitors at the Taj Mahal in Agra for example seemed to be as curious about us as we were about them.

"They come from every far corner of India to visit this mausoleum," explained the guide, "so for some of them, seeing a Caucasian person could be a once-in-a-lifetime experience."

Some wanted to shake hands with us while they tried a tentative, grinning "hello!" We were asked to pose for their photos.

"It would be funny if Dad was here," said Amy. "When they got the shots developed someone would point at Dad and say, 'Who's this?' and the person would say, 'Oh, just some guy I met on holiday in Agra!'" All our children have a very healthy view about their father's celebrity, although they did take great exception to the line in Robbie Williams's lyric that goes:

> *Me. I'm into serial monogamy*
> *Not some bird*
> *Who looks like Billy Connolly*

When one travels west from Agra, one is approaching the desert and the fabled cities in the county of Rajasthan. Here I was reminded of the coloured illustrations in my *Children's Old Testament* that I enjoyed long ago — except for an occasional Coca-Cola sign the sights became thoroughly medieval and relentlessly picturesque. Here would be a five-year-old turbaned drover moving his herd of scrawny goats to a better patch of grass; there would be a group of women with water pitchers or bundles of large twigs on their heads. We began to see pompom-bridled camels along the road, first one or two, and then scores of them, hauling carts, and donkeys with cloth-tied bundles on either side of their saddles. The road became even more of an animal thoroughfare, as sheep and other livestock were herded to market, sometimes a hundred or two in one flock. They were hurried by shepherds wearing bright orange or pink turbans, the East India version of highway safety wear.

We were all intrigued and shocked to see trained sloth bears performing beside the road, dancing on their hind legs while chained and muzzled by their owners.

"We must not stop," warned the driver. "Such people should not be encouraged. It is an illegal practice to train the bears, but when the government offered to swap land in exchange for the bears that only spurred people to breed the bears in order to secure even more land."

Monkeys too became more numerous, and the white cows began to look less well fed. The patches of grass where they could feed had become infrequent, and drinking holes were scarce. Even from our air-conditioned vehicle we could tell that the temperature was escalating, and the devastating result of the drought was unmistakable. The "Lakeview" hotel where we stopped for a pee could no longer boast even a trickling pond. The people too seemed different. They reminded me of the nomadic tribesmen I'd met in Nepal. Men now wore two earrings, which excited Billy when I showed him, since he has sported that look on and off since the sixties. The women's style of dress changed from saris to long, full skirts, short tight

139

blouses and headscarves, all in electric, clashing colours such as lime green, orange and fuchsia pink.

Billy loved their dress sense.

"Now you're talking!" he remarked approvingly when he saw the photos. "Those people know a thing or two about colour coordination."

At Fatehpur Sikri, a starkly beautiful, deserted sandstone city that was formerly the royal capital of Akbar the Great, we gazed upon the highest gateway in the world. The Buland Darwaza, a combination of both Hindu and Muslim styles that towers to one hundred and seventy-five feet, was built by Akbar to commemorate his victory over Khandesh in Gujarat. We were shown a huge squared courtyard where chess was once played using harem girls as the chess pieces.

"You see, the harem girls existed just because they were lively, and brought fun to the palaces," said the guide.

"Yeah, right," I replied, wandering away from such bullshit to photograph a nomadic woman with a beautiful red, mirrored bodice, orange cloak, twenty-eight bracelets, six silver and gold toe-rings, four shiny earrings, three pearl and enamel necklaces and a very large gold-and-ruby nose-ring. She pumped water from a well then carried it off in an earthenware pot on top of her head. That's the thing I could never get used to: no matter how humbly women seemed to live, they were always able to look utterly gorgeous in shimmering saris and superb jewellery. I felt such a slob in my khaki trousers and cotton shirt.

It was in Jaipur that we wilted the most from the heat. It was supposed to be the monsoon season, but we'd seen almost no rain, and the air was dead-dry and heavy with dust. Carrying umbrellas for sunshade, we rode to the glorious Amber Fort on painted elephants, observed by eager *banjas* (bamboo fiddle) players, snake charmers with wicked-looking cobras peeking out of wicker baskets, puppet salesmen with dancing red, purple and gold costumed dolls. A man sat in a shady corner selling mysterious yellow, orange and burgundy coloured spices.

"Ooh . . . Seeing that makes me want to go for the extra fiery Goan prawn curry tonight!" exclaimed Billy, desperately wanting to join us. "Fuck the repercussions!" Billy is a Madhur Jaffrey aficionado from way back and cooks a mean *thali* himself. I had asked the London jeweller Theo Fennell to make a special "curry set" for his birthday: a can of Irn-Bru (that's a bright orange Scottish soft drink that is nothing to do with citrus), a loo-roll holder and toilet brush, all in sterling silver. The funny thing was, I was becoming more and more fond of curry myself, especially the sweeter, northern dishes made with coconut and sultanas. The girls and I, however, craved the foods that were no-no's in this diarrhoea zone: salad, fruit juices with ice, and cut fresh fruit.

One must always be on guard here for potential dangers. A petite grey monkey crouched by an ancient marble column carved with lotus petals.

"Cute!" cried our girls.

"Rabies threat!" cried their protective mother.

A lovely garden covered in vivid pink bougainvillaea led to a palace reception area entirely covered in gold-edged mirror work, inlaid semi-precious stones, windows of intricate wooden fretwork, and even some touches of primary-coloured Venetian glass.

"I want my room to be like this," announced Scarlett. Her father's daughter.

The southern Rajasthan city of Udaipur is set in the lush Girwa Valley. Its translucent man-made lakes were half-empty due to the drought, but the Lake Palace, a two-hundred-and-fifty-year-old royal summer residence that is now a hotel, was still reflected in calm green waters and gleamed in the morning sunlight as we arrived to a fanfare of drums and the strewing of rose petals. Udaipur means "city of sunrise". It was built by the Maharana Udai Singh II in 1567 and is a fantastic combination of desert town, centre for decorative arts, and rock 'n' roll hang out.

"There's a picture of one of the Rolling Stones in the gift shop, Dad," announced Scarlett. "Wearing exactly the same crazy brocade coat we bought for you."

"Oh, bollocks," sighed Billy, desperately trying to tune a bulbous, traditional Indian multi-stringed musical instrument we'd bought at the market place in Agra and Fedexed back to him. We had taken a three-wheeled rickshaw to the bazaar in search of painted silk Indian shoes with curled-up toes, decorative wooden bangles for the girls, and a silk sari for me. Quite a few rupees lighter, we had come back with three bamboo flutes, an Indian nose harp and a banged-up sitar.

"Are you going to make it to Udaipur?" I asked.

"I doubt it," he replied. "This fucking thing's still got me all in knots."

I hoped he was talking about his sitar and not his back.

"Are you any better at all?" I enquired. We had talked for years about going to India together. It would be so terribly disappointing to both of us if he did not make it.

"I don't think so," he said. "In fact I may be getting worse. I'll try to meet you back in Mumbai. I'm sorry, Pamsy. You know I'm dying to join you. Enjoy it for both of us and keep sending me pictures."

In the stunning City Palace complex, where the present Maharana, or King, of Udaipur now resides, we dawdled for hours in the queen's quarters of several centuries ago. Mirrored walls and coloured glass window panes bounced shimmering prisms of light from surface to surface, creating an ethereal and luminous effect. One room with giant silver and red zigzags was entirely mirrored on every surface, apparently a protective device for spotting visitors' concealed weapons. An immensely feminine pale jade painted reception room with floral ceiling murals and a mirrored baby-swing drew gasps from our girls, while an enchanting small eggshell-blue harem room had a black and white striped floor with a chequerboard painted in the middle. Bright yellow walls were edged with forest scenes depicting the adventures of marauding elephants, while a giant gold-faced sun was flanked by pictures of women whose gold-trimmed saris were so delicately painted on transparent paper we were tricked into thinking it was fine cloth. There were blue and white Chinese tiles, mosaic-work peacocks, inlaid precious stones, spires of amber glass, smiling lion murals and a painted cupola ceiling of pink and green lotus flowers. I had always thought I was rather an adventurous decorator, but this entirely put me to shame.

In the entrance hall we saw the lines of descent for this royal family painted on the walls. The names and dates of the rulers were proudly displayed.

"But why only men?" I pouted.

"Even fifty years ago the names of women were not disclosed," replied our guide. "They were known by the family name instead."

He told us an extraordinary story of a mistress of one Bhim Singh, a man who ascended the throne of Udaipur in 1828. Bhim had a few wives, as well as a number of kept women, but one mistress in particular (whose name of course is unknown) considered herself to be as close to him and as important as any wife. Upon his death, she announced her intention of committing suttee, a now-outlawed Hindu tradition of jumping on a deceased husband's funeral pyre, to join her lover in death. His family, however, would not allow such an honourable fate to befall her, since she had not been officially married to him, and they banned her from the cremation ceremony. In response, she first placed a curse on the family, decreeing that generations to come would not thereafter be blessed with sons. She then went to her own home and, at the exact moment of the dead king's cremation, apparently burst into flames herself, unaided by any external fire source.

I was intrigued by this account of human spontaneous combustion, and tried to get some historical verification of the event. I was told it is written down in the *Vir Vinod* history of the Kings of Mewar state by a historian called Shamal Dass. In fact, the curse was fulfilled and boys had to be adopted by the family for several generations.

"But what of the spontaneous burning?" I asked, terribly excited. I had heard about these rare events in human history, possibly with a psychological basis. "Was that actually documented in some way?" I persisted. I failed to get a definitive answer.

"Pamela, give it a rest!" Billy was far less taken with the story. "This Dass guy was put in charge of writing the family's history. It's just like western historians. They make it up as they go along so they don't get sacked."

Despite his eternal pragmatism, Billy was mightily affected by our discussions of the Indian culture, especially the notions of birth and death. In just twenty days the girls and I had become quite desensitised to the street-sleepers, the pitiful approach of beggars, the horrid sights of limbless people, the putrid stenches, the filthy fruit stalls and the relentlessly insistent hawkers . . . yet somehow it felt more like we had gained, rather than lost, innocence.

"There seems to be a lovely acceptance of the order of things over there," Billy remarked, finally standing up straight after a prolonged series of spine adjustments, heat-treatment and acupuncture. He tried on the smashing brocade coat we brought him from Udaipur and admired his reflection on the kitchen window. "At first you think that life is as cheap as a chapatti, but eventually you realise that's only because death, and where that's supposed to take you, is so precious to them. It's a wee bit like Catholicism with a few extra perks, like karma. I hope that stuff's all true. I'd rather like to see my old kindergarten teacher Sister Philomena coming back as a camel. It's really made me think more about a few things. For example, I suppose I'd better pay more attention when I'm fishing. One of them wee trouties just might be Hank Williams."

CHAPTER
SEVEN

Not Giving A
Saggy-Arsed Fuck

When Billy awoke, one summer morning in 1970, he sensed something was not right. He glanced at Iris, his wife, who was still sleeping heavily beside him. Her long, dark tendrils of hair wound their way around the pillow, patchwork quilt, and discarded items of clothing that still cluttered the bed from the night before. He thought proudly for the umpteenth time how much she reminded him of Cher, the lanky American singer. Cher had the same hair and look as Iris with a low, raw voice and wild, sexy outfits. All his friends were crazy about her.

It had been a good night, last evening, and he had the sore head to prove it. It had begun with a gig quite close to his flat in Paisley. It was one of the last ever performances of The Humblebums, a folk group that, after a couple of reincarnations, was now comprised of himself and Gerry Rafferty. He sighed as he thought about splitting up with Gerry, a decision the two men had made a week before standing awkwardly together at Queen Street Station. Gerry was on his way to real

147

stardom, they were both quite sure about that. An extraordinary songwriter, he was already talking about his first solo album. Billy's fate, however, was not so certain. He knew he was talented, the audiences told him that long before he teamed up with Gerry, but what should be his next move? Replace Gerry and continue with The Humblebums? Form another band? Try to make it on his own as a folk singer?

Something else was nagging at him. He smiled to himself as he remembered a moment from the previous night's show when he'd decided to tell the audience a funny story he'd heard in the Scotia Bar at lunch time. What a thrill it was to see people just explode and lose control of their bodies. Maybe he should tell more tales and play less music when Gerry was gone. There'd be no one to stop him, and at least it'd give his fingers a rest . . .

It was quiet. Far too quiet for an early morning with a toddler in the house. Billy hauled himself off the floor mattress and groaned as a wave of pain and nausea hit him. A strong, chemical odour hung in the room. He massaged his head for a second or two then scrambled for his overcoat in a darkened corner. As he did so, he began to notice something different about the bedroom floor. He stumbled to the window and pulled aside the tacked-up red and green striped Navaho blanket that served as a curtain, allowing soft Scottish summer light to seep into the flat.

It was then that he saw the first few, tiny, turquoise footprints, forming a figure of eight at the foot of the bed. They were new, wet and a little smudged. He followed their route with his widening eyes, and realised they formed a purposeful path covering every bit of the bedroom then out through the door. Gingerly planting his own feet in between the paint, like a stork avoiding sharp rocks in a Florida stream, he made his way out into the living room/kitchen, a self-decorated space with orange and purple walls on which Billy had created an abstract mural with polystyrene cut-out shapes. The turquoise footprints walked over carpet, rugs and the low chairs Billy had redesigned by sawing off the legs. One of the chairs had not only been footprinted, but was now almost entirely turquoise-striped. The television too, had become turquoise, and so had the oven, coffee table and refrigerator. The perpetrator, perfectly turquoise himself, in babygro with paint-soaked feet, stood happily on a kitchen stool, near-empty paint can at his side, putting the finishing touches on to the kitchen walls.

It was a good thing they were only squatting there. The little man turned to greet his father with a gummy smile.

"Eh, Jamie," said Billy encouragingly, pointing to the cat. "You missed a wee bit."

Billy reminded his son James of his early artistic endeavours as he was embarking on a career in film set design. James now works and lives in Los Angeles where he is actually paid to decorate rooms in turquoise, pink, green, or anything else he fancies. I feel blessed that he continues to live near to us and visits at least once a week. On the other hand, for most of the year we are bereft of Cara, Jonnie and Walter, who are Glasgow-based.

In the wake of my Hijra studies in India, I began to read about another group of transgendered people, the *fa'afafine*, who come from Samoa in the South Pacific. As I researched the island and people, I was very taken by their culture that is based on close-knit, extended family systems where members live in close proximity to each another. Each family nucleus can be quite large, with a flexibility in structure to allow for informal adoption of cousins, either temporarily or permanently. Reading about this sociocentric culture made me think more, and with a good deal of regret, about our society's egocentric style that seems to lead to separation, loss and loneliness for so many people.

"We should all live close by each other for ever," I announced.

"Mom, you're such a hippie!" said Daisy.

I learned that the *fa'afafine* had carved out a special niche for themselves in Samoan society as nurturers. Being biologically male, yet identifying and behaving more as females, they do not marry or have their own families. That means they are available to stay in their home of origin and care for their elderly parents, uncles and aunts. There is only one institution for elderly people in the whole of Samoa (a population of 150,000 people), because most are cared for within the families themselves. Unlike the transgendered people I treat in Los Angeles, who are mostly shunned by their families, the *fa'afafine* seemed to have found a way to earn tolerance through taking on such an important,

150

caretaking role. Most interestingly, they also seemed to embrace both their male and female aspects.

I was becoming more and more excited about the prospect of beginning my *fa'afafine* studies, and couldn't wait for the time when I'd be free enough to visit Samoa. There was, however, an awful lot to do before I could get away to the South Pacific, in particular, Billy's birthday celebration which was almost upon us. We headed for Candacraig, our Scottish Highland home. Candacraig (a Celtic word that means "the head of the rock") is a dwelling of pale stone, turreted in the Scottish baronial style. In prehistoric times, Candacraig probably was a fortified wooden castle, atop a castle mound called a motte. The wooden structures of the time did not survive, of course, because enemies could easily burn them to the ground, so stone was eventually used. Some elements of the original sixteenth-century building still lie somewhere within the walls of Candacraig today.

When we bought the place from the Roddick family some years ago, I was anxious to know more about its history, so with the help of a couple of professional historians, I began to search for clues. Just as we embarked on this investigation, an American woman whose surname is Anderson wrote to me to ask if she could have a wedding photo taken in the grounds of Candacraig. She explained that, as a child growing up in the United States, she had always been entranced by the painting of Candacraig that hung in her living room.

151

"I was told it was the fairytale castle of my ancestors," she explained, "and I always wanted to see it for myself."

The estate of Candacraig was indeed granted to the Andersons in 1520 by people called Elphinstone. The first record of a Laird of Candacraig is of a Patrick Anderson of Candacraig in 1570, and it remained the ancestral seat of that clan for many generations until the mid 1800s. It's hard to know exactly what Candacraig looked like back in the sixteenth century. The earliest painting of Candacraig dates to the seventeenth century, and shows an elongated stone dwelling without any evidence of fortification.

During the Jacobite period, the estate was held by the 6th Laird, Duncan Anderson of Finnlaylost, an avid supporter of the Jacobite cause. The Anderson family's connection with the locality was severed after three centuries when the 13th Laird, Alexander Anderson of Huntingdon, Quebec, sold the estate in 1866 for £30,000 to Sir Charles Forbes of Newe, who later sold it to Alexander "Dandy" Wallace in 1900.

Like so many ancient buildings, Candacraig was renovated and changed over the centuries, so by the mid nineteenth century it was an enormous, eclectic, castellated structure, with Norman-style towers and circular turrets. It sprawled over what is now the front lawn and its exterior front entrance was an imposing arched vestibule. In 1950, a disastrous fire broke out in one of the corner turrets, and the entire façade, as well as around forty rooms of the southern exposure, were destroyed. Dandy Wallace and his family had been

152

playing bridge when young Alistair Wallace raised the alarm. "I don't wish to disturb your game," he said politely, "but the house is on fire." They attempted to save a Bechstein grand piano signed by Arturo Rubinstein, but it got stuck in the doorway, preventing anything else from being evacuated. The Wallaces later undertook the redesigning and reconstruction of the façade and all the southern elevations, so that Candacraig subsequently became the classic Highland retreat it remains today. It was sold again in the 1970s and then changed hands repeatedly up to the time we bought it.

Our girls were a little dismayed to hear that the ghost of Candacraig is a headless dog. The four-footed spectre is said to have occasionally been seen ascending a tower stair after dark. I must say, the atmosphere does seem odd and somewhat colder in one of the back turret staircases. At times when the girls and I are jetlagged, over-tired and roaming round in the early hours of the morning, we can be quite fanciful about a chance sighting.

"Rubbish," says Billy, "you're a bunch of crazies."

One of the most serendipitous aspects of becoming the owners of Candacraig is its long association with the march of the Lonach Highlanders, and the local Highland Games. The Lonach Highland and Friendly Society was founded in 1822, largely for the preservation of Highland Dress and as a benevolent institution to support local members. Every year around two hundred men in full Highland regalia, with sprigs in their bonnets and pikes in their hands, complete a six-mile walk. Led by flag bearers and the men and women of the Lonach Pipe Band, they make no fewer than five stops for a dram, or shot of whisky, on the way. It is a lump-in-the-throat moment every year when the beautifully polished, brushed and bedecked band of marchers arrive at the Candacraig gates. The Lonach Highlanders are rightly proud of their heritage. Their colours were blessed by Queen Victoria when they marched to Balmoral in 1850, and she mentioned them in the journal of her Highland life. Apparently, as they were leaving, Balmoral fishing ghillies gave them lifts on their backs over the River Dee, presumably so their regalia would not become too soggy.

At nine in the morning on Lonach Day each year, we first hear the Lonach men coming up the glen, a thrilling, haunting sound of pipes, drums and marching footsteps that draws nearer and nearer. The pipers are the first to march up the drive, around three dozen of them in the green and black dress kilts of the Gordon Highlanders, with tall black busbies and shining plaid brooches. They are followed by the clans — men of the Forbes clan, in pale green tartans and black jackets and the brightly clad Wallaces, their red and black kilts swinging in time to the drums. Behind them are a group of Highland marchers from a mixture of clans, and then a horse and cart arrives, led by Willie Gray, a local poet of the Doric language. When I first arrived in the area I asked what the cart was for.

"Och," I was told, "it's to carry the pikes if any of them get broken." I've heard whispers that over the years it was used to ferry along anyone who failed to remain upright after all that whisky, but perhaps that's just legend.

After the marchers have formed a circle in front of the house, their leader, Sir Hamish Forbes, MBE, MC, the Patron of the Society, gives the order for them to stand at ease with a command that tickled us to pieces when we first heard it: "Assume a lazy posture!" He then makes a toast to the householder and Billy replies that they are all most welcome and gives them a laugh or two. Three loud and lusty cheers, and they are on their way to the next station. We look forward every year to this outstanding, historic ritual, and invite friends to enjoy it as well.

When we arrived at Candacraig at the beginning of July, we were hoping for some relaxing family time before Billy's party, but that's not what happened. First of all, the rabbits had taken over the Candacraig lawn. The little buggers were munching everything in sight, and simply didn't care. They hardly even bothered to hop away when we approached.

"We should breed them," suggested Billy. "Is there any easier way to earn a living? When the sun comes up every morning, just shout, 'GO!' "

Secondly, three hundred humans were about to descend upon the place for Billy's sixtieth birthday celebration in mid-August. I was going to be a tad busy.

Doctor and Doctor Connolly
Request the Pleasure of Your Company
To Celebrate His Sexageniality
And His
Not Giving a Saggy-Arsed Fuck Thereof

People had been thus summoned, in entirely over-the-top posh invitations of gold-embossed script on heavy, ivory Smythsons of Bond Street card. It was only after I arrived in Britain in 1976 that I learned such invitations are known in upper-class British circles as "stiffies". In Australia, where I was raised, a "stiffie" is something quite different. I'll never forget a British acquaintance asking me if I'd received a stiffie from her friend Oscar. I told her I was not in the habit of talking about my sex life, and in any case it was none of her business whether the poor man's penis worked or not.

Michael Palin was one of the first to reply. I had mistakenly omitted to mention his spouse:

Are wives invited? Helen is no trouble and I could keep her largely out of sight.

A timely tip-off arrived from actor and author Stephen Fry:

I ought to warn you, I dance like an electrocuted pig.

The Programme of Events was to be as follows:

Saturday 17th August:

6:30p.m.   Highland Welcome: Wee bevvies on the lawn. Pipe Band

8:00p.m.   Dinner and Special Address to the Haggis

10:00p.m.   Dance a Wild Jig

Midnight   Stovies and Champagne: Bare-Bum Cavorting

Dress: Formal, Black-Tie Kilt, or Windswept and Interesting

Sunday 18th August:

12:00 noon   Caledonian Brunch. Address to the Quiche

Afternoon   Fishing, caber-tossing, gorge-walking, cycling, hiking, abseiling, banjo-playing or shootin' the breeze (Warning: All golfers will be fucked and burned)

4:30p.m.   Afternoon Tea. Address to the Scone. Falconry, archery, punting, pontificating . . . or a vicious game of croquet (Glasgow Rules. Full contact.)

7:00p.m.   Barbecue, campfire and music. Address to the Sausage

11:00p.m.   Tall tales and outright fabrications. Address to the Nightcap

Dress: Jeans, Breeks, or Rumpled Intensity.

Billy's birthday was not the only major family event that summer. In 1999, just after she gave birth to

Walter, Cara had been inspired to try to trace her mother. Billy's ex-wife Iris had moved to southern Spain after their marriage collapsed, and over the years her children had lost contact with her. Although I had been Cara's adopted mother for twenty or more years, and had even been present at Walter's birth, it was understandable that she nevertheless had a yearning to contact Iris now that she too was a mother. Iris was eventually located, but Cara's most profound joy was the rediscovery of her grandparents with whom she'd always felt safe.

"They're mad!" She laughed affectionately on the phone. "They're living a Glasgow life in a Mediterranean country. Football, Lotto and Guinness. They've even kept my glass animals for me. Grandma's just as much a hypochondriac as ever!"

Helen Pressagh had been delighted to inform her long-lost granddaughter of her latest self-defeating triumph:

"Cara! I'm nearly blind!" she announced, followed by, "I've got a new cat called Misty!"

"Why did you call her Misty?" asked Cara.

"'Cos I can barely see her!"

In fact, her health truly was abysmal, and sadly she lost her sight and her life in very short order.

She and her husband Bill had spent most of their married life in the once-industrial town of Clydebank, just outside Glasgow. Bill was a quality controller in the field of light engineering at the Singer company, where Billy's father had worked just after the Second World War. They had two beautiful daughters. The elder,

158

Nessa, became a dentist, but in the early seventies she contracted breast cancer and died within a year or two. Bill and Helen were devastated by their loss, and the collapse of their second daughter's marriage to Billy was another great sadness. When Iris moved to southern Spain, they fretted about her welfare and finally followed her there. They were a kindly, unsophisticated couple. Helen's brother Sam was married to a woman called Ella. When Billy turned up at family gatherings where Sam and Ella were present, he relentlessly called them "food poisoning", but they never got the joke.

James reconnected with his grandfather just a few months after the death of his grandma. He barely recognised Bill Pressagh, who was himself suffering from cancer and seemed in great need of better medical attention and personal care. James shared his concern with me by telephone, and disclosed that he and Cara were trying to figure out a way to help him. I was worried about the situation, but it was tricky for me to intervene. Eventually I received a worrying phone call from Cara.

"We've decided to kidnap Granddad," she announced. "He's not being looked after in Spain."

"Does he want to leave?"

"Yes, and we really must get him out of here," she explained. "We'd like him to spend his last days in relative comfort."

So the exhausted, frail and dying man turned up at Candacraig on a windy summer's day at the beginning of August, just two weeks away from Billy's birthday party.

"Hello, Mr Pressagh." I was shocked at the state of him. "You're very welcome here."

He scowled at me, and I wondered if he still blamed me for the demise of his daughter's marriage a quarter of a century ago. Granddad settled into an armchair with an oatcake and a cup of tea in which to dunk it. He was tiny, hunched and wizened, the skin stretched tightly over the bones of his skull. He seemed terribly weak and undernourished. His voice was so thin and his Glasgow accent so thick I could barely understand him. I'd met him once in the mid-eighties but he was entirely unfamiliar. Everyone in the family took turns to sit with and care for him. We all felt great compassion for him, but at the same time we struggled with the fact that he was, in reality, a stranger to some of us. There was an odd atmosphere in the house, and everyone was out of sorts. Billy's nightmares seemed to be even worse than usual, and one night he accidentally punched me in mid-sleep combat.

"Who were you attacking in your dream?" I asked next morning over Vegemite toast.

"Julie Walters. She was being a prick. Can't remember why. Shame, 'cos I like her in real life. She's jolly. Remember when she came to our place, drank wine, and thought she was an aeroplane?"

"We'll have to go back to building the Berlin Wall," I said. "I've got bruises on my arms."

"The Berlin Wall" was created nightly between us with a pile of pillows, whenever Billy was going through a period of having particularly violent post-traumatic nightmares. People who've had devastating experiences tend to symbolically revisit them in their dreams, and Billy is no exception. I usually watch him thrashing around and ranting unintelligibly until he drifts into peacefulness, although I occasionally have to intervene in order to avoid calamity. In fact it has been less problematic since he was diagnosed with sleep apnoea and was introduced to the C-PAP breathing machine. In anticipation of a good night's sleep, he now dons gear resembling that of a deep-sea diver.

When Billy first sought medical advice about his sleep disorder, the doctor advised him to try sleeping on his side. After a week or two, Billy reported that such a position was impossible for he always rolled over on his back.

"Do you have a T-shirt with a pocket in it?" asked the creative physician. "Wear it to bed back to front and put a tennis ball in the pocket. That way, if you roll on your back you will be so uncomfortable that it'll prompt you to turn sideways again."

Billy followed his advice but, in his true lateral thinking style, substituted an apple for the tennis ball.

"That way," he explained, "when I wake up in the morning I've got breakfast."

This method of snore-prevention, however, did not work, and instead he received an electric breathing machine and mask that would force air into his lungs. It turned out to be a far better option than the apple, and he began to have far more restful nights. Being Billy, however, he initially had some technical difficulties.

161

"Oh, press my wee grey button, would you?" he asked me when he woke one morning.

"I love it when you talk dirty." I said.

Even Walter was acting out the tension in the household. That night, as Granddad anxiously watched television coverage of a Glasgow football game, the rest of us ate dinner to the percussive sounds of the one-year-old tearing around the kitchen banging every metal surface he could find with a steel spatula.

"He was worse earlier," said Cara. "He went stir crazy after eating Chinese food. All that MSG . . ."

Billy plonked his best shot of the moment.

"You mean 'stir-*fry* crazy'!"

No one took any notice.

"Och, I thought that was rather good," sighed Billy.

We were all anxiously protective as we observed Granddad attempting to move about the house. He was wonderfully stubborn and refused most offers of help, but in truth the steep and numerous stairs were far too challenging, and even simple activities like dressing or bathing completely wore him out. Chewing was problematic for him because his dentures dated back to the fifties, so we brewed soups and stews to try to encourage him to fortify himself. After a few days of this, he did begin to eat better. His eyes began to sparkle a little, and he seemed to be walking slightly faster. He sporadically engaged in conversation with the family, and even talked about moving back to Glasgow when he was better.

"I've never had an excuse to wear a kilt before," he said brightly, when we talked about the party. "I'm

162

looking forward to it." His hopefulness was encouraging, and we thought he might continue to improve. Cara and James were wonderfully attentive, and the old man was clearly grateful to them. They sat patiently listening when he rambled nonsensically, ran his bath and coaxed him into taking his medications.

"I'm so proud of them," said Billy, with tears in his eyes.

But it seemed that each step towards health was followed by more set-backs, and it soon became clear that Granddad needed more help than we ourselves could give, we asked a registered nurse to provide additional care. She swished around in her crisp uniform, gracefully handling his alternating grumpiness and provocation.

"I can't believe it!" cried his grandson. "He was actually flirting with her!" I gently pointed out that younger family members are often shocked when they notice signs of sexuality in elderly people, but that they should darn well get over it. In my work setting I have often come across such judgemental attitudes towards older people. It always seemed to be worse if the person was suffering from chronic disease or disability. I wish we could all let go of such prudery and ageism, for sensuality and sexuality are known to improve a person's quality of life no matter what their state of physical health might be.

The weekend after he arrived, I helped Granddad stagger outside into the walled Victorian garden and seated him comfortably in a warm, windless corner. He sat hunched and shrunken, utterly dwarfed by a bed of colossally overblown blue Himalayan poppies. It was one of those rare and breathtaking Scottish summer's days we get in the north, when soft sunlight bounces between trout-rippled loch and sapphire sky. I tried to draw his attention to the miraculous sudden appearance of a lovely black iris but he was languidly disinterested and kept asking if we had any gladioli.

"Not really." I was puzzled until Billy later told me that Granddad's prize glads had been the talk of the leafy Glaswegian street he'd eventually abandoned for a bleached hacienda in Benidorm. He haltingly reminisced about picnics and hiking by Loch Lomond, then drifted away to a deep silence. It was his very last day in the sun.

CHAPTER
EIGHT

Carping The Diem

It was a grey and drizzly Saturday morning in Partick, the kind of weather Glaswegians describe as *dreich*. Cursing at his difficulty finding things in the dim tenement, Billy hurriedly pulled on his black jeans with green zippered back pockets, grabbed his bomber jacket and ran for the bus at the bottom of Stewartville Street. As he leapt on board the crimson double decker it took off at a startling pace, almost flinging him back off again on to the concrete bus shelter. He clung to the platform pole for dear life until he found the equilibrium to stash his fishing rod carefully under the circular stairs and collapse into the nearest downstairs side seat. He breathed deeply and took a look around the dingy interior. A couple of older lads were smirking at him from further down the row of double seats on the opposite side to him. Wankers. He ignored them and dug in his pocket for change. The conductor was lurching purposefully down the aisle towards him, steadying himself by grabbing metal seat-corners with one hand and the ceiling rail with the other.

Billy wondered if he could get away with paying a child's fare. Turning seventeen had been a severe drain

165

on his pocket, but he was small for his age and could often pass for younger. He shrank lower in his seat.

"Half fare, please."

"Pass?" demanded the conductor, unswayed by his acting. Billy shrugged his shoulders.

"You're no sixteen." The conductor himself was just a teenager. He'd played the same tricks a couple of years back and knew a scammer when he saw one. Billy pleaded the contrary. A child's fare would mean the difference between being able to buy some decent bait or not.

"I am, right enough." Billy looked at him pleadingly. It worked. He settled delightedly back into his seat and checked that his equipment was still safe. Billy's approach to fishing had been very hi-tech from the start. Bits of string and safety pins had been all very well for other boys, but he had started off with a square metal slotted holder, with the line wrapped round it, which he used when he first started fishing during summer holidays in Rothesay. Now he had graduated to a rod: an impressive, telescoping metal contraption that had been adapted, in typical post-wartime fashion, from the discarded aerial of a military tank.

Once upon a time, Billy had used the tongues of black mussels he found in the Clyde as bait. He thought that was dynamite stuff, until he found something even better. Now his chosen bait was the very best a boy could come up with after an extensive period of research and experimentation.

166

"Eh, a tin of Spam, please, and some frozen dough," he said to the grocer when he alighted from the bus in Clydebank.

"Killer bait!" the grocer nodded approvingly. "But not together, not a sandwich."

Billy staked out a bit of canal side, attached some Spam to his hook, and began to cast. He dreamed about catching a pike, but despite his rich bait he usually caught only perch and roach. One day he'd fish in the sea and catch cod, or even venture to the still water ponds to catch carp. Billy was intrigued by the stories of carp fishermen, who fished the still ponds to which he had no access. Titanic things, carp. He'd heard of the black variety growing to three or four feet long, and weighing forty pounds. His casting neighbour from the previous week had told him a story about two men, Alec and Jimmy, who'd cast away at a pond all morning, waiting for a single bite.

"You know, I don't think there's a bloody fish here," said Jimmy, very disheartened.

"I can assure you there is," snorted Alec. "I caught a forty-five-pound black carp here."

"What?"

"Yes. A couple of years ago."

"Bugger off."

Silence.

"Then I'll tell you the biggest thing I caught here," countered Jimmy. "I was casting away, and I decided to fish a sinking line. I was fishing quite deep when I felt a colossal tug. I hauled it up, and so help me, it was an

167

enormous copper lamp. Not only that, but the candle was still lit!"

"That's a load of rubbish," scoffed Alec. "Who do you think you're kidding?"

"Well, I'll tell you what," said Jim at last, "I'll make a deal with you. You take ten pounds off the carp and I'll blow out the candle."

As he grew older, Billy lost all interest in carp. He never ever caught one, and came to view them as desperately indulged fish with exotic tastes that seemed to escalate. Once they were content with sweetcorn or luncheon meat, but by the time Billy was in his twenties he noticed that tackle shops carried bait called *boilies*, round sweets flavoured with mango, grapefruit or raspberry. The carp fishermen would buy these delicacies and sit on covered camp beds for their entire holidays, maggots on their left and sandwiches on their right. They even got fitted out with electronic sensors, in case the fish took a bite when they were sleeping. Billy thought those men must be on first-name terms with some of the big beauties they caught.

Billy says the carp eventually ruined canal fishing. The Singer Sewing Machine factory at Clydebank had a large pond for cooling machines where carp began to breed. At some point the residents of this ever-increasing colony were released into the canals, where they ate all the available food and grew even bigger. People got wind of this and began catching them in ridiculous numbers, often taking them home and keeping them alive in sinks and buckets.

No matter what Billy catches, he continues to be thrilled by the moment of making contact with a wild creature. It is the same as flying a kite, feeling something alive and uncontrollable in his hand, with the sensation creeping up his arm. Whenever something from another world announces itself, his heart goes "whoop! whoop!"

"When a human being gets the first message from outer space that's exactly how it's gonna feel," he says, awe-inspired by the very idea. "Tug tug ... Fuck, they're here!"

Nowadays Billy is passionate about fly-fishing, but he is also keen on variety. He once enjoyed ice-fishing, when the BBC deposited him on an Alaskan iceberg for a documentary survival film, and is intrigued by those nighttime casters in Australia who go out in the daytime to catch worms that live in the surf. They stand in the water with a nylon stocking filled with some old fish and roll it in an arc in the returning wave. When the worm then pops its head up they use a credit card to squeeze it against their thumbnail so they can pull it out of the sand.

"It's the only known occasion," says Billy, "where people use fish to catch worms. Sure proof that Australia's upside-down."

Billy recently had an opportunity to go bonefishing in Mexico, to make an American television fishing programme. Billy, James and the programme makers flew to Cancun and drove three hours down the Caribbean coastal side of the Yucatán peninsula. Billy is very blinkered when it comes to a fishing trip.

"How brilliant," I said when he called and told me where he was. "You got to see the Castillo at Tulum?"

"The what?" he asked.

"Billy," I said, consulting a Mexican guide book. "You landed in Cancun and drove south. The most fantastic Mayan ruin on that whole coast is down there. You passed it. Tell me you saw it."

"You mean that big pyramid thingy?"

"Yes, absolutely that big pyramid thingy. A thousand-year-old thingy with amazing frescos. Didn't you get out of the car for a look?"

"No," he said, stifling a yawn. "It was full of tourists."

I was intrigued by the picture of the Temple of the Frescos, with its extraordinary celestial friezes featuring two-headed serpents and "diving gods". Uppermost on my husband's mind, however, were rather, "diving bonefish".

"Tell me about the journey." I was struggling to understand.

Not far out of the airport, Billy and his gang hit a dirt road that continued all the way to Boca Paila. There was little to see, apart from screening hedges, palm trees and cacti, so they stopped only once, for water. When their people-mover came to a halt they found themselves at a small lodge by a gorgeous stretch of pristine beach. They settled into sparsely furnished stone bungalows with thatched roofs, from which they could see white beach dotted with sandpipers, stretching for miles in either direction. Before them the water was pale jade green as far as a curved reef, thereafter deepening to dark emerald. Silenced by the beauty of the place, Billy ate some home-cooked chicken for dinner in a communal dining room full of dedicated fishermen with hearty appetites, then went to bed.

The next day he was taken out in an open, flat-bottomed boat with an outboard motor, to where the elusive bonefish dwell. The creatures hide in what is known as the flats, very shallow sandy-bottomed inlets with a rocky border that lets the sea seep through to the mangrove swamps. Further off he could see some deeper, cooler salt water channels through the mangroves where bigger fish live, and lagoons with dark holes that lead underground to the sea. There are manatee down there, awesome, prehistoric-looking creatures that resemble legless, swimming cows.

Billy called me from the flats that first day.

"How's the fishing?" I asked.

"I saw a four-foot piranha."

"You what!? Four foot!?" I cried. "You don't go in the water, do you?"

"Yes, but I avoid wearing anything shiny . . ."

We lost satellite connection before he could correct himself.

"I meant *barracuda*," he said, twenty-four worrisome hours later. He could always tell when one of those swimming swords was lurking nearby because there would be a sudden rush of mullet all leaping out of the water trying to fly.

"It was a shame," he says. "I like mullet. They're fish with a bad haircut. Achy-breaky fish."

171

Billy was entranced by the birdsong he could hear emanating from the mangroves, and wished he could match the sounds to the birds: beautiful black-headed gulls with orange-red beaks, black cormorants with scarlet throats, huge brown pelicans with yellow foreheads, and the blue-footed boobies.

Bonefishing seemed to require the use of specially designed flies, sometimes inch-long pearly-pink contraptions called *gotcha* with two silver eyes at the front and long feathers flowing back from the head. Mostly the fishing party utilised some beautifully made crab-like designs that were deemed best for bottom fishing. Billy stood either in the water or on the boat in his ankle boots, shorts and polarised sunglasses, trying to cast so that his fly landed slightly in front of the bonefish. Then, with a short tugging motion he would pretend his fly was a small creature lying there on its sandy bed to entice the fish to snap it up.

"The guide sees the bonefish first," says Billy. "You never see them. It's the same as the trout spotters in New Zealand. I'm always saying, 'My God, how did you see that?'

I loved Billy's description of bonefish. They seem to be the most clever and illusory creatures who have three different appearances: ghostly, mirror image and dark. In reality they have the same shape and muscly firmness as mackerel. At those times when you think they're dark, you're actually looking at their shadow. That's really how you catch them: find their shadow. It occurred to me that many miles apart and in different settings, Billy and I were engaged in very similar activities. From his description, bonefishing and psychotherapy seemed very much alike, only I fish for the human shadow.

Landing the bonefish was just as challenging as spotting them or enticing them to take a first bite. Apparently they take two or three long runs of a hundred or so yards. If you're unlucky, they'll run into mangroves and get your line all tangled up. The protocol for the programme was catch and release. Billy found the fish was very tired by the time he landed it, so he had to spend a bit of time holding it in the water until its strength came back. Otherwise, it would be consumed by a predator.

On the very first day out, Billy caught one of the dark-skinned permit fish, a trickster with a tail so wide he looks bigger than he really is. Billy spotted his dorsal fin peeping above the water like a periscope and managed to land him forthwith. According to local fishing lore, if you catch a permit, bonefish and tarpon all in one day, that's called a Grand Slam. Billy managed to land a permit and a bonefish on the same day, achieving something informally known as a Slim Slam. A fisherman who catches all three plus a snook achieves a Super Grand Slam plus a ridiculous amount of glory.

All in all the team spent about seven hours a day on the water. In the early evening they would rest, shower, then eat dinner together and shoot the breeze.

It was a very male environment. The only women around were those who worked at the lodge.

"What did you guys talk about?" I enquired nosily. I really shouldn't have asked, for it's none of my business. The male societies he inhabits are mysterious to me, and I actually like it that way.

"Och, fishing and absolutely everything," replied Billy. "The moon, stars, sea, motorbikes, cars, and travel. Where we'd been and things we'd seen."

Billy tried to avoid getting caught up in the "I caught a bigger one than you did" mentality. He is disinterested in competitive fishing, and finds big game catching quite obscene.

"The people who do it all look like golfers to me," he says, "golfers at sea. All golfers should be fucked and burned."

By mid August, Billy was forced to face the fact that a number of golfers, all nevertheless close friends, would shortly be arriving on his doorstep. His particular brand of logic led him to feel perfect justification for a bout of extreme cantankerousness. "Whose fucking idea was this party?" was his rhetorical rant the morning the scaffolders arrived to create a level flooring and balcony for the most ridiculously huge party tent any of us had ever seen. At Candacraig, whenever Billy feels impinged upon by me or the world at large, he will disappear to the loch. It is his refuge, his solace, and frankly the best place for him when he's crotchety. He had wandered down there in an attempt to escape the hollow, resonant banging and ringing thuds as heavy poles were off-loaded from a giant semi-trailer that was now blocking his customary view of the gorgeous Donside valley. After only half an hour or so he returned and stood exasperated, hands on hips, at our front entrance. The words *Carpe Diem* were carved in stone above his head.

"How's a man supposed to catch a wee troutie with that din in the background?"

"They'll be a few days, I'm afraid." It was actually more like ten. I winced in anticipation of the inevitable explosion. "Why don't you take a trip down to Glasgow? I'm sure there must be a football match or something . . ."

"Och, I don't fancy that. Walter's here."

Billy strode off with his grandson to play in the furthest corner of the garden by a small pond with a three-foot island in the centre and a tiny waterfall. It is a child's idea of fairyland and, moreover, a small drooping willow on the island provides a perfect hideaway for a toddler. In the spirit of enhancing the elfin quality of the haunt, Billy had purchased some garden gnomes and placed them near the pond. When I first saw them, I was hopping mad.

"There's kitsch and there's revolting kitsch," I complained. "Your snow globes are fine but the gnomes definitely aren't."

Billy was undeterred. The grotesque little creatures irked me every time I passed, but the more I complained, the more they seemed to multiply. Mysterious FedEx packages began to arrive with "FRAGILE" written on the side. Then one day, I sneaked down to the fairy pond where I caught him red-handed, creating an entire gnome colony. He looked ridiculously guilty when I approached, attempting to appear nonchalant while planting a gnome with fishing rod in a prime bank-side position. I knew I was utterly beaten.

"Billy," I said, pointing to a girl-gnome, riding pillion on a tiny red three-wheeler, "is that your secret bit of stuff?"

Only Granddad seemed oblivious to all the noise of the rising scaffolding. He sat in his wheelchair, all spruced-up by his night nurse, staring vacantly at his side plate. James had recently purchased his sky-blue pyjamas and elegant dressing gown, but no one would have regarded him as a man to paisley silk born. I wondered where his mind had taken him now. Walter occasionally commanded his attention for a second or two, but then he would disappear back into his morphine haze.

"So this is what it's like," I thought to myself. "When you're near the end, your skin shrinks, your eyes recede into your skull, and everyone tells you you're looking great. Death's the elephant in the room."

Granddad drank a little tea (everyone in the family knew just how he liked it now: lots of milk and three or four sugars) but Cara discreetly mashed his scrambled eggs in vain, for he was now beyond food.

"He'll not be long," the nurse had decreed knowingly the previous evening. "Once they stop eating it's all but over."

"I hope Granddad makes it to the party," said Daisy. "He could get to meet a Beatle." But the celebrations were hardly For the Benefit of Mr Pressagh, and

Granddad was not in a party mood. In fact, he was becoming paranoid and delusional. "They're trying to kill me," he whispered when I took my turn at his bedside.

"Who is?" I asked in alarm, but he hadn't got a clue.

Cara and James made a new appointment for him with a specialist in Aberdeen.

I loved their optimism, but I knew I was going to have to talk to them about letting go. I knew from experience that at some point dying people really need to have loved ones' permission to go to their rest. To me, Granddad looked pretty well ready for his final journey.

Down the hill in our local village, Canadian people from the Squamish Nation were carving a totem pole that they had been invited to erect in the vicinity. They had begun in April through the vision of a local man named Kenny Grieve who received a Millennium grant and a gift of wood from the Balmoral Estate. The pole incorporated designs suggested by local school children, who in turn took their inspiration from local legend, folklore and nature. A salmon and osprey were emerging at the top end, and an owl was forming halfway down. Local folk were encouraged to help, so under the guidance of the master-carver, Xwa-lack-tun, I took up a long-handled chisel and began to chip away at the wing of the owl. The carving action was soothing to me, almost meditative. It gave me a chance to think more clearly about the runaway train that the birthday event had become. Was it really the right thing to do, especially with Granddad so ill? I felt great empathy for

177

his suffering, but at the same time he had never really been part of our whole family. What if he passed away right in the middle of the event? I felt terrible for worrying about the effect that might have on the party, but it seemed to be a legitimate concern. I had recently heard a macabre story about a woman in Beverly Hills who had organised a lavish dinner for her husband's birthday at a swish restaurant. In the middle of it, he showed signs of having a stroke but she downplayed it in front of the guests. Someone called an ambulance, which sat outside while they finished dinner at her request. "Hell," she was heard to say, "I even had a facelift for this party!"

Then there was the most important question of the birthday boy's own feelings. He was becoming more and more agitated. Gifts were beginning to arrive, some more welcome than others. The people at Age Concern sent him a T-shirt, and someone had the audacity to send a birthday card with someone impersonating his own voice. I had presented him with the ultimate gift for a true hermit: a splendid gypsy caravan, marvellously colourful with red, turquoise and gold painted exterior panels and a fully operational interior. It even had beds and a kitchenette where he could make himself a nice cup of tea. Fortunately, he loved it . . . and now, there was a thought: perhaps he could be persuaded to move in there for the interim?

My own stress level had also been rising. I had taken to writing myself frantic notes, saying things like "borrow more folding beds" and "toilet paper/guest towels?" But now it seemed the whole raison d'être for

the event was in question. On the one hand I believed
Billy should be celebrated, after all his extraordinary
achievements that belied his early hardships . . . but on
the other hand he himself was entirely ambivalent
about it. I understood that there was still a part of him
that thought he deserved little, and it was right for me
to oppose that. Then again, I was worried that we'd
only been able to invite a fraction of all the people we
would have liked to include. Those who had accepted
the invitation were relatives, school friends from his
days at St Gerard's in Glasgow, men who'd started
their welding careers as sixteen-year-old fellow
apprentices, folk singers and heroes, teachers, gamekeep-
ers, gardeners, tour promoters, footballers, rock 'n'
rollers, actors, comedians, writers, fishermen and
neighbours. It was wonderful to have such a
cross-section of people from every part of his life, yet it
was turning into such madness that I began to wonder
if maybe after all something much smaller would have
been better. And what if it all went horribly wrong?
What if people didn't turn up? What if the tent was a
disaster? What if it poured with rain? What if the place
caught fire? What if? What if? What if?

Out of the peaceful swish, swish, swish of my carving
instrument, the half-formed owl seemed to speak to
me. "Take it easy," she said. "Breathe. All will be well."

Back at Candacraig, the tent people were noisier
than ever. So were the entertainers I had hired to
re-enact a fifteenth-century clan battle for the
enjoyment of guests of all ages. Several very authentic,
woolly-looking people turned up and pitched two large

medieval tents by our tiny loch. They set up a colourful working camp, complete with braziers, fires, flags and weapon stands. Celtic chests, baskets, furs and stone jars decorated a central cooking area, while a blacksmith created swords in a forge tent. Unkempt male creatures in breeches, plaids and battle helmets threw themselves into savage training exercises, preparing for a "fight to the death" between two stunt teams using spears and double-headed axes, halberds, claymores and basket swords. The camp followers prepared food for them on ancient-style griddles: broth, ribs, chicken, bread and bannocks (oatcakes) served in crude pottery bowls that seemed likely to cause lead-poisoning. Everybody loved them except Billy, who continued to see the whole exercise as an irritant, interfering with his fishing.

It was during one of my sorties to check on their doings by the loch that James found me with the latest bulletin.

"They're sending an ambulance," he said. "Granddad's to go into hospital."

"Wouldn't he prefer to die here?" I asked. "We could cope."

"I don't think that's an option."

"Rubbish," I said, but there was no point in any of us arguing. Apparently it's tidier if you oblige people by dying within spluttering distance of a mortuary. Perhaps it would just be more comfortable for him in hospital, but in any case no one was going to make a fuss, least of all Granddad. For a couple of days Cara, James and Billy took turns visiting him in a place of brusqueness, wall-rosters, chrome beds and strip-lighting, until the St Andrew's flag on the Candacraig battlements was finally lowered.

"Billy's Flag at Half-Mast in Memory of Elvis Presley!" announced the tabloids.

On the day of the party, Dame Judi Dench arrived just before lunch time.

"Come and see the tent," I urged her.

"I've already seen it."

I looked at her in disbelief.

"This morning . . . in the newspaper."

I had thought I'd heard a helicopter before breakfast. I rolled my eyes and led her inside some flapping canvas doors to a staple-gun world. Soon every inch of the white tent walls would be covered in the tartan of Billy's mother's clan, MacLean of Duart. I love the tartans associated with both Billy's maternal and paternal clans. For this occasion we'd chosen the predominantly scarlet dress tartan contrasted by the hunting MacLean, one of the oldest tartans in existence. The latter dates back to the sixteenth century. It is a simple dark green sett with black and white grid stripes.

In my previous writing about his maternal relatives I spelled MacLean without the first "a". I was subsequently challenged by a cousin or two.

"But you read the book before it was published," I complained to Neil MacLean, "so why didn't you mention it to me then?"

"Well," he said sheepishly, in the obliging way of many Scottish people, "you wrote such a nice book and all I didn't have the heart."

I asked Billy why he didn't tell me and he admitted he gets confused about the spelling. Neil says this is because the name was misspelled on a plaque outside Billy's grandfather's house and no one ever bothered to change it!

Billy's paternal tartan is McDonald of the Isles, a lovely bluey, pale jade green sett that is associated with several variations on the Irish name Connolly. People from other cultures often find it hard to understand the nuances of these meaningful tartan designs, and the relationship to clan and family. I once overheard one of Scarlett's American school friends, who had noticed a framed photo of her wearing a dancing-kilt, exclaim, "Hey . . . they make you wear that in your tribe?"

Billy himself pooh-poohs all the fuss about who's entitled to wear which tartan. "It's all nonsense," he insists. "Tartan was invented by a couple of Jewish guys in Edinburgh in the nineteenth century. You can wear whatever the fuck you like." Once upon a time Billy despised people who wore the tartan. As a child he would watch for the swinging pleats to swish by and sing out "Kiltie, kiltie cold-bum!" Of late he has discovered that he is content and comfy wearing traditional Highland dress, and I must say I love to see him in it.

I assume that the "couple of Jewish guys" Billy was referring to were the infamous Sobieski Stuart Brothers, impostors who claimed to be related to

Bonnie Prince Charlie. I recently learned that they produced a forged book called the *Vestiarium Scoticum* that presented details of tartans that were supposed to date back several centuries. There is disagreement about when tartan-wearing actually began. Some take Virgil's line *"virgatis lucent sagulis"* or "they shine in striped garments" as proof that Celts were wearing clan tartans back when Christ was alive.

The Scots did not always wear kilts. Although much disputed and debated, kilt-wearing itself is thought to have begun around 1594 when a group of Irish mercenaries came to Scotland wearing a form of the "belted plaid", the original wraparound kilt. It was just one large piece of cloth that acted as blanket, towel, garment, hood and pocket, held in place with a belt and plaid brooch. You had to lie on the ground to put it on.

The modern pleated, tailored kilt made from a minimum of four yards of tartan probably evolved from the plaid in the late eighteenth century. It seems extraordinary that the wearing of the kilt was banned by the government in the Dress Act of 1747, after the '45 rebellion. That decree was not repealed until 1782, by which time many customs and traditions associated with the kilt had been lost. Fortunately, traditional dress became very fashionable after the Highlands were romanticised by Sir Walter Scott. King George IV wore a kilt on a visit to Edinburgh in 1822 — and he started the new rage in earnest. Good old Queen Victoria loved to see a man in a kilt and insisted that all clan chiefs should wear their tartan when they came to visit her. In some cases the chiefs didn't have one and it had to be

183

specially designed. Nowadays there are thousands of tartans, and people are constantly inventing new ones. I once designed one for Billy, but sadly he didn't approve. I incorporated lime green and shocking pink, but perhaps there wasn't enough purple.

As for the sporran, that was originally just a plain pouch. Being a psychotherapist, I should probably know why men would want to have a huge hairy sack dangling between their legs, but frankly I have no idea.

The pièce de resistance at the entrance of our marquee was a massive polystyrene statue of Billy that truly looked like it was made of granite. It was a fantasy, supposed to be Billy as a great engineer, though it looked like a socialist statue, with Billy grasping a spanner, flanked at his feet by a small Scottish terrier. It had been fashioned by props-makers for the Camelot commercials.

"Well, that's it finished," they said when the filming was over. "Don't know what we're going to do with this thing now. You want it?"

"Sure," said Billy. "I'll phone the wife. Maybe we can stick it in the garden for a laugh." So we had it hauled up to Scotland where it sat in the garage mouldering away for months until I decided to use it to help decorate the tent. As a piece of trompe l'oeil, it was really quite convincing. After the party, Billy's friend Russell Kyle reported that he had met a bagpiper in Glasgow who said, "I saw you at Billy's party. Brilliant. But this success thing has gone to his head."

"What do you mean?" asked Russell.

"That fucking statue!"

"That was polystyrene, you bampot," retorted Russell. "I saw Billy lifting it with one hand."

In fact, Billy hates to see grand images of himself in the house, unless they're tongue in cheek. We have an over-the-top, gilt-framed photo of him in full Glasgow Police Band tartan uniform, under which is inscribed *Our Beloved Leader*, and Cara's friend and artist Gareth Reid has painted Billy as *Magnus Barelegs*, a conquistador *sans* trousers. There's a rather nice bronze bust of him in the hall on which little Wally has planted a Bob the Builder's hat. Billy thinks it looks much better that way.

"Some famous guys' houses look like a shrine," he says. "It's the worst thing you can do to your children. I prefer my home to be a shrine to them. I like to see *their* pictures all over the place instead."

As Dame Judi and I negotiated an obstacle course of step-ladders, guitar-leads and power tools, I noticed my heart was beating awfully fast. Would it all be ready in time? Judi must have been wondering the same thing, for she most endearingly asked me what she could do to help. Waiters scurried around draping large round chipboard tables with stiff ivory cloths. A tribe of harried-looking women were wrestling masses of sunflowers into a vibrant cacophony of cheeriness, while others stuffed tall ivory candles into candelabra fashioned by a local blacksmith in the shape of Clyde-style engineering cranes. The birthday boy stood just inside the interior marquee entrance, staring in bewilderment at two giant flower-filled banjos now adorning the stage.

"I wish we could know when Armageddon will be upon us," he glumly wished out loud.

"Why?" I enquired, a little alarmed.

"So we could accelerate the spending."

Billy is terrified of spending money, especially on himself. Time and time again throughout the process of preparing for his party I had to remind him that he deserved to have a lavish celebration for this important birthday. He is a charitable man who has given much to others, and this was a time for self-generosity. I had to concede, however, that he did have a point, since such events have a tendency to gain a momentum of extravagance that can panic even the wealthiest host. Unforeseen scenarios kept cropping up. It had been a massive task, for example, to arrange for hundreds of people from all over the world to make their way to the Scottish Highlands. "Billy," I had said at one point, "we're providing transport to and from the hotels. You don't think we'll have a problem getting people off the premises once the party's over, do you?"

His silence led me to look up and seek an answer from his face. It was covered with an ominous smirk.

"You don't know my friends."

It was partly true. He'd hidden some of them from me . . . or perhaps there just hadn't been enough opportunities for me to have met them all. I'd spoken to many on the phone . . . but that's not the same as facing a well-soaked person whose legs no longer function sufficiently well to climb aboard a hospitality

186

vehicle. My imagination went wild. I could see our lawn dotted with battle-weary, half-kilted legless folk in the post-party dawn.

"Let's hire a couple of stretchers," I resolved, "and those beefy caber-tossers from the Highland Games."

The menu was easy. We would serve Scottish fare, including haggis, a traditional offering made of oatmeal and sheep's offal that is usually served with great ceremony. It is accompanied with "neeps and tatties" or mashed turnips and potatoes, and I think it tastes pretty good, especially with whisky poured all over it. After reading Dickens, Billy wondered if it might be the Scottish version of "umble pie", an English dish made of deer's offal that was given to servants in earlier times (that's where the expression "eating humble pie" comes from).

The haggis is bagpiped into the room in a formal procession. Then, the nondescript little grey sausage is solemnly addressed with a nineteenth-century Robert Burns poem called "Address to a Haggis", complete with mimed burping, spewing and blood-thirsty actions that result in a vicious slashing of the great pudding with a sharpened knife. The whole ceremony is quaint, curious, brilliant and fierce all at the same time.

Then there was the question of the birthday cake. Jane Asher kindly offered to make Billy one of her fantastic edible designs, but we didn't think we'd manage to get it up from London in one piece. Billy traditionally receives a loaf of bread with a candle stuck into it, a meaningful hark back to the first time he ever saw a birthday cake, flaunted by a clown at the circus.

"Look!" he cried at six years old. "He's got candles in his loaf!" I considered giving him a large bread loaf with sixty candles on it, but that would hardly feed the five thousand. I perseverated far too long, then finally a local cake designer fashioned a wondrously colourful, six-tiered contraption that was so large it also fed the dedicated staff at the Aberdeen Royal Infirmary where Granddad had spent his last days. It had to travel there in its own van.

There have been some wonderful cakes over the years. In 1999, when Billy was on tour in Australia, he and his promoter Kevin Ritchie and Steve Brown his manager were all given birthday cakes reminiscent of some aspect of the tour. Billy's had dolphins because he had been lucky enough to swim with the wild creatures off the Western Australian coast. Steve's depicted an underground stream in Sydney known as the Tank Stream, while Kevin, who is known to engage in compulsive ironing as an anxiety-reducing pastime, received a dessert-sculptured iron and ironing board.

"I don't know where to start," said Kevin, overwhelmed by its ingenious details. Billy's sound engineer Malcolm Kingsnorth set him straight:

"The collar, I believe."

People began to arrive in the Highlands three days before the party. The New Zealanders and Australians arrived first, hoping to shake off their jetlag early in the crisp Scottish air. Every hotel and bed-and-breakfast establishment in the general area had been booked out, and several kind neighbours had offered their own homes for billeting guests. It was thrilling to be able to

188

introduce such a wide variety of people to the extraordinary beauty of the Scottish Highlands. As our guests made their way to Candacraig on Saturday evening, the magnificent, deserted hills between Ballater and Donside were aflame with the late afternoon sun, and gloriously wrapped in heather. Tiny stone bridges spanned icy cold trout streams and brooks, all abundantly decorated with ferns and wildflowers. On the summits they could spot stags with perfect antlers silhouetted against the deepening sky, while smaller roe deer leapt across the narrow passes, right in front of the vehicles. When people arrived, they were greeted by a Highland welcome from the bagpipers and musicians from the Lonach Pipe Band who played, among other offerings, a tune their leader Pipe-Major Alistair Laing composed for us called "The Connollys of Candacraig".

Billy and I greeted guests at our front door, he in his kilt and I in a blue satin evening gown with a painful bodice. We were both showing signs of stress.

"Why do you always wear clothes that are too tight for you?" asked Billy.

"Why don't you just come straight to the point," I snapped.

After signing the Birthday Book the guests battled their way through the amassing throng to a covered marquee entrance further along the hallway. The interior of the marquee was now a vast tartan cavern, glowing with candles. Spotlights bounced off crystal, silver and traditional studded Scottish targes, or shields. Sunflowers, being Billy's favourite flowers along with daisies, were everywhere, in vases, on walls, and strategically placed at the nape of each tartan-swathed chair. At one end of the room a large stage had been prepared, while in the centre was a massive and intricate frozen rendition of Billy's vroom-vroom dream: a Harley Davidson motorcycle ice sculpture dripping ever so slowly into a metal tray. Few people lingered inside the warm tent, however, choosing instead to wander out through French doors to a newly created balcony at the other end of the marquee. There they could have a "wee bevvie", or pre-dinner drink, and gaze out at the magnificent, sunset-bathed Don valley. Those who dallied to chat on the lawn were rewarded by the sight of arriving acquaintances, and frequently took aim with a well-considered taunt about their unfamiliar, kilted appearance. Most Highlanders consider it a compliment when visitors wear Highland dress. A few incomers, however, had put their kilts on back to front, or their accessories in the wrong place, which only added to the merriment. Everyone wanted to know what garment, if any, lay beneath each kilt.

The dinner placement had been an impossible task. I finally decided that after a socially correct seating for the first course there would be a lottery, a kind of egalitarian mission in the form of musical chairs. On arrival, a guest was given an initial placement, then randomly drew two seat numbers (men and women drew from separate hats). After the starter, a cry of "all change" sent people careering round the room to find their next place and dinner partners. The same occurred after the haggis was bagpiped in. It was delicious to see Billy's Glaswegian folkies making friends with princes, marchionesses prattling with lefties, American movie stars chortling with Billy's sister Florence, and his old welding chums arguing belligerently with newly minted rock stars. Many were wearing the purple goatees they'd found in tartan-covered crackers beside their plates. Some people had mislaid their tickets by the third and last changeover, with hilarious results. At one point, Bob Geldof ended up at the children's table, which apparently didn't bother him.

The haggis was addressed in the traditional manner by trades unionist Jimmy Reid, a beefy, immensely likeable hero of Billy's who became one of the most powerful and respected spokesmen of the working class in Scotland. During an economic downturn, Jimmy refused to let the shipyards close, and encouraged the workers themselves to take over the running of the business. His plan was successful and thousands of jobs were saved. Billy made a special trip up to Rothesay to visit him in recent years, and they have been friendly ever since. The haggis was addressed for a second time, in brilliant extempore fashion, by comedian Robin Williams who titled his offering "Ode to Haggis and Fiery Bums". People just screamed, and I was relieved to notice that at last our guests were relaxing.

After dinner, Billy gave a little welcoming speech. I have never seen him so truly overwhelmed with emotion before a large crowd. He expressed his profound happiness that so many people he loved were all together in one room, then touchingly paid tribute to Bill Pressagh, who had just been cremated in the kilt he'd hoped to wear on this occasion. Billy also spoke of the pride he felt towards James and Cara for their brave, loving care of their Granddad. The cake appeared, borne aloft by brawny Highland men, then everyone sang happy birthday.

When it was time for the dancing, Billy and I kicked it off with a tentative round of "Gay Gordons", followed by a more wacky, diverse line-up for "Strip the Willow" than I'd ever seen. A recent study showed that Scottish reeling is good for the psyche, but Celtic people have known that for centuries. "Strip the Willow" is an exuberant line-dance that defies centrifugal forces. I saw a legendary drummer whirling precariously with Billy's little niece Julie, and a femme fatale rock star galloping with adoring young Californian males, more accustomed to board shorts than their dashing, flashing kilts. Sir Hamish Forbes, eighty-something-year-old wartime hero and illustrious leader of the Lonach marchers, pranced bemusedly with an LA valley girl, while an elegant Lady took a turn with a waltzing welder.

At midnight we served stovies, Scottish dumplings traditionally made with left-overs. Billy's cigar-smoking cronies gathered in a smaller, British Raj-style Indian tent to shoot the breeze and play music, while one immensely talented guest offered private solos of hit songs in the drawing room for scores of lucky people who serendipitously wandered in at the right moment.

The following day, everyone returned for brunch (in jeans this time), then wandered around the grounds chatting, making new friends, watching the clansmen battle by the loch. They fished, punted, and strolled in the gardens. Many took their turn at flying the beautiful falcons, eagles, buzzards and other exquisite birds of prey that were presented that day by local falconry experts. Some preferred to relax in the marquee playing instruments, while others discovered the authentic Native American teepee we'd erected in a sheltered woodland area of the grounds and took a fireside nap on sheepskin rugs.

By afternoon tea time everyone seemed to have new best friends, and there was a lovely sense of heightened congeniality, good-humoured bantering, and downright silliness all around. As I traversed the lawns I overheard tantalising snippets of conversations I had no time to join in. "I can't wait till I'm sixty and have my own castle!" quipped an American screenwriter. "I've never learned to fly-fish at a party before," exclaimed a slightly soaked satirist.

A much-admired Scottish actor best reflected my own feeling. "Bliss was it on that lawn to be alive."

We heard of enchanting moments that occurred even before the party began. For example, two New Yorkers, who had last seen each other at a script conference in Toronto a week earlier, had walked out of their hotel rooms at exactly the same time, and did simultaneous double-takes to see each other unexpectedly standing there in full Highland regalia.

As evening fell, we all congregated around a huge bonfire in the woods. A wonderful Irish pub band played superb Gaelic folk music and they were joined by some of Billy's musical heroes, Ronnie Drew and Paul Brady. We warmed ourselves with grilled prawns, sausages, and toasted marshmallows, and watched the sparks fly upwards into the navy twilight sky. Everyone said the crack was fierce, which is Glaswegian for the conversation was scintillating. Billy's *Timeline* pal Anna Friel sang a haunting song with a purity of voice that made our hair stand on end, before some gentle rain began to fall between the lofty cedar branches.

No one would have viewed the pyrotechnical display in dry clothing had not Cara and Jonnie thought of having umbrellas made to serve as party-favours for every guest. They designed the perfect black-and-white striped brollies with Billy's hairy face on four sections. When rain began to pelt down towards the end of our barbecue, people simply unfurled them so they could comfortably follow the torchlight procession of the Lonach Pipe Band and assorted "medieval" clansmen to a higher vantage point. The fireworks began whizzing to the sounds of Billy's hit "If It Wasne For Your Wellies", then soared to the theme from *The Archers* radio show, a tune that Billy has promoted as an alternative British National Anthem. Finally, Billy's bearded visage appeared in full catherine-wheel splendour to Loudon Wainwright III's growly rendition of "Happy Birthday". The totem-pole owl had been right after all. I really couldn't have asked for things to go any better. It was such a relief, and best of all, the birthday boy was ecstatic.

"All in all," he said later, "I don't like birthday parties, although I don't mind other people's. I found I absolutely loved my party, which took me by surprise. The house looked fantastic and the tent was brilliant. If I walked properly, I could avoid the bits I didn't much care for. I liked absolutely everybody who came. It was an extraordinary feeling, being with friends from childhood, from my youth, music and drama . . . from all the departments of my life. They were all linked by the fact that they were my friends and had remained my friends. Many of them had enriched my life, and some had even changed it. That made the atmosphere very extraordinary. To have so many delightful people I love being in one place with me was heaven. I only wish we could have invited more."

"What did you like the best?"

"Och, to stand in the wood and listen to delightful music; to warm myself at the fire and tell funny stories with my pals. To see Paul Brady blowing people away . . . a lot of people had never heard of him and were completely flattened. Ronnie Drew telling stories about Dublin that they'd never heard. It was wonderful stuff, and not really showbiz . . . far more real joy to watch them. And Martin O'Neil was there! People dancing and laughing at the fire . . . and to watch Geldof being so proud of the Irish band because they were so outstanding . . ."

He went on and on, and I was very glad. Billy's sister Florence got it exactly right:

"Billy," she said at the end of the evening. "You certainly 'carped the diem'!"

Billy's friend and producer Phil Coulter encapsulated the thoughts of many long-term pals:

I was bursting with pride for you as I stood outside your fairytale castle on Saturday evening, listening to the pipe band welcome a succession of the great and the good — and I couldn't help asking myself, "Is this the same Billy Connolly who, thirty years ago, was told that people would never understand him outside Glasgow?" I think the begrudgers have been well and truly fucked!

CHAPTER
NINE

A Tsunami In Partick

They were a couple of nutcases, him and Alec Mosson. As fellow apprentices in the shipbuilding trade at Stephen's Shipyard, they were always up to some kind of mischief. Both eighteen-year-old newbies, Billy had begun his apprenticeship in the welding field, but Alec was now a plater, one of the workers who align the large plates of steel that comprise one section of a ship's hull before the welders came along in their rawhide leather jackets, goggles and oxyacetylene torches, all ready to join them up.

Alec was a scrawny boy, a little shorter than Billy, with wavy auburn hair. He lived in Anderson where his father worked on the dockside. At fifteen years old he had started work in the Kelvinhaugh Street boiler shop for the Barclay Curle Shipyard, but after a couple of years he went to finish his time in Stephen's Shipyard where he met up with Billy. The two teenagers already knew each other slightly, through evening sorties to the F and F's Ballroom in the Dumbarton Road in Partick, and lengthy cider drinking sessions at the Sarry Heid bar. Now workmates, they would sit at lunch in the shipyards with other apprentices, fabricating tales of

197

their previous night's success with women, known as "getting a lumber".

The foreman had learned from bitter experience that he needed to keep his eye on Billy and Alec. They were the ones most likely to be lighting farts below deck, redesigning people's work clothes, or buzzing them with electrical equipment. The pair of renegades were eager to do anything bar work, and were quite ingenious in their extra-curricular pastimes. They would throw light bulbs into the Clyde from the forward end of the ship, then scamper aft to chuck nuts and bolts at them to try to smash them as they floated past. When the tide was in, they would have competitions with other apprentices to see who could throw a welding rod into the murky water and make the smallest splash. At first they thought this was a fine game that could be surreptitiously played; however, the retreating tide later revealed hundreds of tell-tale pieces of evidence, all stuck firmly in the mud.

On a slow, windy autumn day Alec, in a spurt of customary creativity, took a piece of chalk and drew the outline of a double-decker bus on the bow of the ship, just below the bridge. It was an inspired piece of madness. The portholes became the bus windows and Alec cast himself as the traffic-wary driver. Sitting there perkily on an oil drum with an imaginary steering wheel in his hands, he shouted "All aboard!" to passing workers. Not one to be left out of a piece of work-shirking silliness, Billy hopped on as a passenger, and the two of them improvised a lengthy sketch that kept fellow workers entertained for an hour or two, until the managers got wind of it.

"Get to yer bloody work," they growled.

Alec had been an ardent Celtic supporter his whole life, but he was hard-pressed to find enough cash to attend a mid-week game. In those days workers had to purchase their boots from the shipyard's company, which then took two shillings and sixpence off a man's weekly salary until they were paid off. Alec, however, managed to utilise a fine scam. He found he could get thirty shillings for his boots from the pawnbroker, which would pay for his football ticket plus a few wee bevvies. Such a practice was not all that unusual — for example one worker pawned his toolbox every week. Fortunately the pawnbroker never bothered to look inside, for the man had replaced all his hammers with bricks. Alec figured out that he could frequently repeat the exercise to great temporary advantage, and enjoyed some fine Wednesdays at Celtic Park. He was eventually paying off at least five pairs of boots.

Then one morning, his foreman turned up to see him.

"Eh, Alec," he said, quietly pleased with his detective work. "How many boots d'you have on your feet?"

When Celtic Football Club gave Billy the very much appreciated honour of a Seat for Life in the grandstand, the then managing director Fergus McCann held a modest function in the boardroom, during which he made a brief presentation speech and Billy replied with words of gratitude. Among the worthies waiting to greet

199

him, Billy noticed a dignified man in his fifties with a familiar, mischievous smile.

"Do you remember me?" asked the right honourable Lord Provost of Glasgow. He shook hands and presented his card to Billy, who was suitably surprised.

"Of course! My God . . . Alec . . . how are you?"

Between displays of passion at their team's play during the next few matches, the two caught up on the past forty years.

Alec was active in politics from a young age. He was involved in trades unions as a lad, then eventually became a shop steward in the insulating industry. As he and Billy continued to catch up on the missing details of each other's lives, Billy found they had one thing in particular in common.

"I stopped drinking on February 8th 1978, by the grace of God," Alec says. "It took me a long time to realise I needed help. In Glasgow if you didn't drink people thought something was wrong. 'You're twelve now,' they say here, 'so why've you not got a drink in your hand?'" The same year he become sober, Alec joined the Labour Party, and twenty years later he had become the Lord Provost.

In July, the River Clyde had burst its banks, which left the east end of Glasgow stricken with disastrous floods. The homes of many people in that area were lost, swept away in the rising, putrid waters.

"That's a hell of a thing," Billy said to Alec when they met just after Billy's party. "All these people without insurance. What can they do? My heart goes out to them."

"Aye," said Alec. "I've been down there all week. There's a Common Good fund but it'll only run to one or two hundred pounds per family. We just don't have enough for a decent shake."

"You've been down there, you said?"

"Aye, but people on the whole didn't want to talk about the floods so much," said Alec with chagrin. "They seized the opportunity to make other complaints."

Alec had listened to their litany of grievances. It hadn't helped that they'd been on the news.

"Eh, what's this?" one man had said. "They're saying we were poor. I heard it on the telly. We're working people, not fucking poor."

Billy was appalled that the news that week was all about floods in Prague, rather than something closer to home.

"Saving nice old buildings is one thing," he said, "but saving people who are in deep shit 'cos the sewer's come up the close is quite another."

He resolved to help. He's a stickler for fairness.

"I love architecture," he said, "but people come first. Screw the art. Seems to me those who rush to save it are the same people who don't mind dropping bombs on it when the situation demands. And if those Glasgow Eastenders don't have insurance, the last thing they need is a lecture that they should have it. Anyway, some companies tell you floods are an Act of God and are therefore not covered. But I can help a little." Billy had made a movie on that theme, *The Man Who Sued God*, about a fisherman whose boat was sunk through a lightning strike and was denied insurance. It helped him to understand the system. So he and Alec formulated a plan: a series of three fundraising concerts that Billy would perform, for which Alec would arrange free use of a concert venue. They chose the Armadillo, a colossal metal structure belonging to the City of Glasgow, in which Billy had performed in the past.

It seemed appropriate that, on those charity concert nights, Billy should recount some of the experiences of the flood victims. They were darkly hilarious.

"Some wee woman," he told them, already breaking into a titter, "someone's granny . . . she was putting a towel under the door. There was a fucking tidal wave coming down London Road, a tsunami has left Partick and is on its way . . . and she's fending it off with a tea towel. There she was, talking to her pal on the phone . . . there's people riding on top of the wave in Argyle Street. She was telling the Provost: 'Aye, I was phoning Agnes on the phone and sticking the towel under the door. I was saying, Aye it was terrible. I've just got the towel down now.' You can see council houses slipping past the windey and she's going: 'That's it under the door.' Her friend, who's two doors down, goes, 'Well, you better look round, Mary, 'cos it's coming in the kitchen window.'"

Whenever Billy retells this, he cannot stop laughing. It's the same as the falling skaters in Park City. "If this happened to you or me it would be hell," he says, "but it's funny the way people falling down a hole is funny, or walking into a pole, or when you see drunk people fighting and they're all missing and falling. That awfulness is nightmarish, but it's also fucking funny."

202

★ ★ ★

In early October, Billy began work on *The Last Samurai*, an epic movie starring Tom Cruise that is set in Japan. Filming was also to take place in Los Angeles and New Zealand, so he was gearing himself to do a good deal of travelling over the next few months. He looked forward to spending more time in Japan. Billy feels simpatico with Japanese people, since he has long noticed that the Japanese laugh louder than anybody at ghoulish humour and unintentional slapstick. They, of course, invented humiliation reality TV shows, truly appreciate body humour, and collapse at farting jokes. In fact, gallows humour appears to be a national pastime, and that has truly endeared them to Billy.

But beyond their humour, Billy intuitively recognises something familiar in the broader Japanese nature.

"They're very like Celtic people," says Billy, "very poetic and gentle . . . yet ruthless at the same time. There is a duplicitous edge. What you see is not what you get. In Celtic culture there's a welcoming face, an attitude to strangers that is brought out and dusted down. In Japan it's exactly the same."

On the eve of Billy's first rehearsal day for *The Last Samurai*, he was a little anxious.

"Want some dessert?" I asked. In perfect keeping with Billy's latest movie job, our family had developed a passion for Japanese rice-covered Mochi ice-cream. "There's green-tea, mango, cappuccino or vanilla."

Billy shook his head. "Nah," he declined. "I've got to rehearse the fight scenes tomorrow. Cruise will turn up all buff . . ."

"Um ... I may be mistaken, darling, but they probably cast you for the contrast ..."

The make-up department had asked Billy to grow his beard as long as possible, with which he was only too happy to comply. In the end, though, it was Tom who got the beard. Billy's was trimmed to a little white goatee and his hair became a nineteenth-century bob. He was excited to become this new character, and began to practise his sword play for some battle scenes.

"I've got a stunt double," he announced proudly the following evening, hoping that would impress. But our girls were eager to find out the details of his first meeting with the movie's star.

"What's Tom Cruise like?" they chorused

"Och," their father shook his head. "He's ridiculously handsome. I fancy him myself."

It was a brave thing to say to a couple of teenagers, but it was intended so innocently he got away with it.

"Did he ask about us?" The unalterable egocentricity of adolescence.

"Yes ... in fact he gave me something for you."

Billy's childhood hero Houdini could not have conjured better delights. Billy rummaged in his leather rucksack, ejecting mouth organ, chewing gum, a copy of the *Banjo Newsletter* and a car-sticker that said "Honk for Jesus". Finally he extricated three chic black baseball caps with the words *Last Samurai Productions* embroidered in red on the peak, in both English and Japanese.

"Eeeeghhhh!" They screamed with delight. "They're so coooool!"

204

A Japanese village had been created on the Warner Brothers back lot.

"It's fantastic!" exclaimed Billy. "They have all these brilliant little Japanese shops. I wonder if they'll let me have the big wooden sandal outside the shoe shop." On an awning above the store was a three-foot by two-foot Japanese *tojo* sandal with a velvet strap between the big toe. Billy thought it was beautiful. He wanted to see if he could have it when the movie people were through, because he thought it would make a great coffee table, but couldn't figure out whom to ask. It was almost the Japanese equivalent of the "Big Slipper", a novelty gift Billy loved to joke about on stage. Several years ago, Billy spotted these furry, two-feet-in-one-shoe comfort items being advertised in weekend magazines and began to talk about them on stage. For him they are tantamount to the beige cardigan in signalling boringness and advancing age, but nevertheless so ridiculous they're funny. He received dozens of them from people who wanted to join in the joke.

With or without a Big Slipper, comfy chair and fire to sit beside, Billy has a tendency to doze off whenever he feels like it. Filming is the perfect profession for a napper, for there's endless waiting around. Some people knit, gossip, play cards or stress out about their next scene, but Billy frequently just passes out. He's also very easy to please. Legends have grown up around the dressing room contract requests, or riders, of stars who demand "a vase of roses *without the thorns*", or "a bowl of M&Ms but *no brown ones*". An all-white room with a white-covered walkway to the stage is the requirement of one female artist, and a yellow rubber duckie that of another. There is a legend about one rock band demanding wheelchairs at every airport in case they were too stoned to walk. Billy's rider requests are tea and water.

Billy was asleep in a rickshaw waiting for the next scene to be lit when Tom Cruise and Steven Spielberg spied him, and sneaked up to wake him, mid-snore, with an unceremonious bang.

"Fancy being asleep when I want to introduce you to Spielberg," shouted Tom. The two were amused to see Billy waking in fright to see such luminaries peering at him. I met the director some years before, when he was looking for a female lead for *Raiders of the Lost Ark*. I had bounced into his office wearing a white T-shirt with fake bloody bullet holes. "It's my John Lennon Assassination T-Shirt," I announced. It may be fine with the Celts and Japanese, but that kind of sick humour rarely goes down well in Hollywood.

Billy continues to enjoy movie making, which I find admirable. I lost interest in the process after a very short time of appearing in B, C and D films. The waiting around, the tension, and the lack of control are all elements that I found insufferable; but for Billy it is a perfect opportunity for him to either sleep or sit quietly and unbothered in his trailer for hours on end, tinkling on his banjo.

After completion of the first phase of filming on the Universal back lot, Billy took off for Japan for the commencement of principal photography. He and I had visited Tokyo five years before, when *Mrs Brown* was shown at the Tokyo Film Festival. We'd both enjoyed the extraordinary juxtaposition of ancient and modern features of Japanese culture: early Shinto temples with meditating monks a few yards from punk teenagers in kimonos made of black bin liners. It was the same on the set of *The Last Samurai*: eighteenth-century Samurai soldiers in full Japanese leather armour and shaved heads with pony tails, sheltering themselves from the sun beneath blue plastic umbrellas while munching doughnuts.

Billy was particularly taken with the complexity of the Japanese armour and weaponry.

"It's as if they decided, 'Right, we're gonna fight each other with swords, so what's the most difficult way to do that? We'll get a hat we have to balance, let's see . . . a bandana with a knot in it! That'll keep us occupied. Then we'll get clothes that are so weird and huge we'll have to keep our wits about us just to stay dressed. And we'll have to tie a bowtie behind our backs just to keep our pants on. Add to that wooden shoes that only come halfway along our feet, and a sword that takes a year and a half to make and costs three years' wages!'"

When you fly to Tokyo from Los Angeles your body clock wakes you at four in the morning. That's a perfect time to visit one of our favourite, albeit weird, Tokyo haunts, the vast industrial cave that houses the Tsukiji Fish Market. We timidly entered this freezing, steamy place one morning and were introduced to an eerie, glowing world in which row upon row of fish stalls display every curious sea creature, alive and dead, that has ever been eaten by human beings. People scrambled up and down the narrow aisles, trying to find the best buys of pearly yellowtail, Atlantic salmon, spiky sea urchins, and even frogs, while the vendors sliced savagely at slimy carcasses and shouted encouragingly at their customers.

Noisy tuna auctions were in progress, the winners bowing modestly to the losers while helpers manhandled the sleek, red-numbered creatures on to waiting trolleys. Some of those bluefins, that weighed over sixteen hundred pounds, must have been flown all night from the east coast of America. A piercing, high-pitched beep! beep! warned us to leap for our lives as narrow, fast-rolling forklifts and trailers nipped past. They roller-coastered up and down the lanes, ferrying the latest victims of last night's sea raid to waiting display tables. Shiny eels with evil teeth, staring shark and puffed-up blow fish were arranged artistically beside fifty kinds of shellfish and a few large squid. Many crustaceans were still temporarily alive in wet, plastic-sided homes.

"What the hell is that?" asked Billy, pointing to a slimy black thing with pointy eyes.

"Dinner, I believe," I replied, having no idea at all. Everyone was busy, enveloped by swirls of icy mist that fragmented the spotlight and created an atmosphere that was so surreal it reminded me of the staged dry-ice dream scenes in old Hitchcock movies.

Gasping for some warmth and sunlight, we ate fresh sashimi for breakfast at an outside stall, then wandered to the Hama Rikyu Garden to take a ferry to Asakusa.

It was lovely to stroll in the peaceful three-hundred-year-old garden after the madness of the market. Wisteria-draped bridges span a beautiful pool where ancient shoguns once stalked ducks, while a river path leads past bird-filled groves, tea houses and picturesque pavilions. We peeked inside one of the latter and found we were just in time for a tea ceremony, the ancient Zen ritual known as *cha-no-yu*. I wondered how Billy would fare waiting such a long time for a cuppa, but he breathed, relaxed, and watched curiously as two women performed the thousand-year-old ceremony with precision and contemplation.

Our journey down the Sumida River to Asakusa took half an hour or so. After the fairly standard embankment view of apartment buildings, warehouses and office high rises, it was startling to see the work of my favourite contemporary designer-architect, Philippe Starck — his golden fantasy building, the Asahi Beer Hall.

"It's the sperm-donor clinic," said Billy, referring to the familiar-shaped emblem on the top. We climbed the stairs and leaned backwards to gaze upwards at the glass façade. It gave me a queasy feeling of reverse vertigo, for I'm funny about heights. I felt much more comfortable in the stall-lined pedestrian lane called the Nakamise-dori, a place for finding treasures such as Japanese dolls, fans, crackers, hair ornaments, and silk material. I bought a small scarf while Billy mucked about in the shoe shop, then we continued on past a sensational five-storey, red-and-gold pagoda that is supposed to contain some of the Buddha's remains.

Eventually we reached the famous Sensoji Temple, the oldest in Tokyo, dating back to the seventh century. It's dedicated to Kannon, the Buddhist goddess of mercy and compassion.

"You want to check your fortune?" I asked, noticing the temple stall where people were shaking bamboo sticks out of wooden boxes.

"Nope," he replied bluntly.

One hundred yen lighter, I was soon the proud owner of a piece of paper with Japanese symbols that no doubt spoke of success and travel opportunities . . . if only I could decipher it. I learned later that there was a translation booth nearby that I entirely missed, and also a place to hang fortunes that people wished to negate.

In October, Billy was briefly based outside Tokyo, in the tiny town of Himeji-shi.

"How is it?" I asked over the phone.

"Japanese TV is terrible," he complained. "You have to go down to the foyer and pay 1,200 yen . . . that's the equivalent of ten dollars . . . to get extra channels to watch. It turned out to be just two extra ones . . . a choice of golf or pornography. The loneliest thing in the world is watching pornography on your own."

I raised an eyebrow. "Really . . ." Maybe I should make a mercy-dash to Japan. Fortunately, there was a "part two" to his statement:

". . . so I watched the PGA tournament right through . . . twice."

Billy throughly enjoyed his work relationship with his fellow actors.

"Tom's a nice man, Pamsy," he said over the phone. "Loves his kids." The actor Tim Spall made Billy laugh with his impressions at tea time.

"My life simply depends on a fondant fancy," he would say corpulently as the catering truck arrived.

According to Tim, it was Billy who managed to break the ice on the set. Tom Cruise is not a man who believes in his own mystique, but being so illustrious there was a hushed reverence on the set whenever he was there . . . unless Billy was around. At the time there was a false rumour being circulated in magazines that as a contractual obligation people working on the movie had to avert their eyes from looking directly at Tom. On the first day, Tom and Tim were on their horses while Billy as the Sergeant walked along beside them. Billy caught Tom's eye.

"I'm looking at you," said Billy, pointedly, eliciting a huge guffaw from the movie's star.

It was nice that Tim, a great hero of Billy's thought his acting was impressive.

"People think, 'Oh blimey, he's just having a good time'," Tim said to me, "but he's done the bloody work like a proper actor and he's always spot on. So few comics can do that. Acting is reductive, and people who are used to being solo performers don't always get it."

"You'd better watch out," I said when I relayed Tim's praise to Billy. "You're getting good enough to become a Brussels sprout."

Billy had very little filming to do in Japan, so he had a chance to embark upon his usual traipsing around. He explored the shops in Osaka, and was amazed to find that some of them actually bore a close resemblance to those he'd enjoyed on the back lot of Warner Bros Studios in Los Angeles.

"The Japanese wrap everything so well," he enthused. "If you buy a pair of socks, they wrap them as if you've just bought a Fabergé egg. Wonderful wrapper-uppers. They just love making it nice for you."

When Billy arrived home at the end of the month we all went out for a celebratory family dinner. Driving home from the restaurant, Billy suddenly screeched to a halt in the middle of Ventura Boulevard. I held my breath as three policemen huddled in a group looked up with anticipatory frowns. "They're going to book him for dangerous driving," I thought. "I mustn't let him take the wheel when he's jetlagged."

But Billy jumped out and ran towards them. "You guys loitering here?" he said accusatorily.

The three officers laughed and embraced him. "Where you been, man?" said one affectionately. They were all cigar buddies. "In Osaka with Tom Cruise," said Billy proudly. "Doing a movie."

"Do you stay alive to the end of this one?" asked another. Billy has been killed off early in his last few films, and it had got to the point where the first thing he did when he got a propective script was count the pages till his downfall. This one wasn't too bad, but he decided to be mysterious.

"Wait and see!" he smiled sheepishly.

The children and I had recently watched a documentary called *The Making of "White Oleander"*, in which we saw Billy actually announcing to the greater American public:

"After I get killed, the movie really takes off!"

Only a man with a true lack of career guile would say such a thing. Among film crews he is appreciated for his eccentricities. On one of his days off at a New Zealand location for *The Last Samurai* he was sitting eating a sandwich in a main street cafe, wearing cotton breeches, Mary Jane sneakers and a bright orange "Jesus is my homeboy" T-shirt that Scarlett gave him.

The director Ed Zwick came walking by.

"Billy," he frowned, "who gets you ready in the morning?"

CHAPTER
TEN

Is There No End To This Fucking Birthday?

It was a mid-seventies jousting tournament, Glasgow style. Billy strolled about the streets after a gig in the Scottish border town of Galashiels, resplendent in a floppy hat with snakeskin band, a tight sailors' Hong Kong jacket, broad-striped flared trousers and glove leather rock 'n' roll boots with high heels. It was his favourite look of the moment, and he had completed it with a huge, gold-hooped earring that a gypsy fortune-teller might wear.

"You're a big fucking Jessie," muttered a brave man in Billy's direction as he passed him on the pavement. The man was fitted out as a Malcolm McDowell clone in *A Clockwork Orange*: painters' overalls, bowler hat, and one huge false eyelash. His jousting stick was a sharpened umbrella.

"Is that right? How would you like your eye done, country boy?" replied Billy.

214

"I'll stick this fucking umbrella into you if you don't watch out," said the man.

"Oh yeah?" enquired Billy. In an instant, he swung his borrowed banjo like an axe and brought it down neatly and most melodically on "Malcolm's" melon. It bounced beautifully, causing his now well-warned aggressor to withdraw lest the instrument be wielded in earnest. Billy stood his ground.

"There. How does the key of 'G' suit you, big mouth?"

Ironically, the Glaswegian slang for thumping a man is "to banjo" him. Billy's five-stringed friend has long been far more than just an instrument for him. He appreciates its ability to take a good old doing, and considers it far more robust than the guitar. But beyond its protective qualities the banjo has provided him with solace, livelihood, and a way out of the shipyards. Small wonder, then, that he continues to be devoted to it, and anyone who finds it irksome to hear the sound of repetitious riffs floating through the kitchen wall at all hours of the night had best keep that to herself.

Billy takes his banjo everywhere he goes in the world, and especially likes to go on holiday with other pleasant people who play complementary instruments so he can jam with them. If those people also happen to be the kind who can make him howl with laughter, he's in heaven. That is why I organised a secluded, music-focused escape for celebrating Billy's real birthday on 24 November.

I chose the one-acre island in Fiji where Billy and I were married. It is a Robinson Crusoe lagoon isle off Suva, a rustically appointed paradise that has eluded the western pace of life. Anxious that everything should go smoothly, I flew one day ahead of him so I could check on final preparations and make sure there were no disasters. It was, after all, hurricane season.

Billy and I have not had good luck where tropical winds were concerned. We once booked a holiday on the nearby Hawaiian island of Kauai. Just before we left Los Angeles, I asked Billy to phone the hotel to check on children's meals. A bemused man answered the phone.

"I'm sorry to have to tell you this," he said ominously, "but the hotel's no longer here."

"What? Are you kidding me?"

"I'm afraid not," said the stranger. "It was blown down last night. I was just walking along the beach when I heard a phone ringing in the sand, so I answered it."

Happily, everything was going more or less placidly, including the weather, on the Fijian island where the final portion of Billy's Sexageniality would take place. Micah, a sweetly smiling and shy fisherman with a left leg ravaged by childhood polio, had spent most of the night weaving crisscrossed palm frond baskets for the welcome gifts of coconut soap, sandals, *sulus* (sarongs), copies of *A Snorkeller's Guide to the Reef* and *How to Say it in Fijian*, a T-shirt and coconut jewellery. Pristine were the fourteen thatched native *bures*, or sleeping-huts, with woven coconut wall linings, each with a palm-bordered slither of grassy beach dissolving into rippling turquoise sea.

Sweating unpleasantly in my floral *sulu*, I waited by the tiny runway at Nausori airport.

"You VIP lady?"

"Not really . . . Oh, OK . . . yeah . . ."

The customs official led me into an air-conditioned room reserved for Pacific Rim dignitaries. The genteel blue and white drapes and climatically useless velvet sofas contrasted with a wall display of wicked-looking artefacts from Fiji's pre-Christian past. A central giant cannibal-fork with four prongs for the easy dissection of human flesh was flanked by one-strike wooden clubs, a massive machete and a couple of pointed dinner catchers.

"The plane's coming late."

"How late?"

"Another hour."

I strolled out to spend time with the other aimless folks marking out the territory between the check-in desk and the noisy International Rugby Cafe, home of orange sodas and bright pink lamington cakes. I was heady with the fragrance of voluptuous, over-laden frangipani trees that lined the drop-off lane. Frangipani are my very favourite blossoms. I stuck one behind my ear (left? right? I could never remember which side signalled marriage) and watched a mongoose darting under and over the perimeter fence. Vans began pulling up beside the kerb, depositing tapestries of Indian families carrying cardboard boxes: kohl-eyed girls adorned with beads, braids, pantaloons and brilliant silken saris, and boys in tunics and woven plastic sandals. I guessed that a prop-plane commercial flight was about to depart for Nadi, and sure enough a DC3 eventually creaked into the air. Its jolly surfer-wave, bikini girl and hibiscus motif, covering a good part of the aircraft, contrasted with the sleek, gleaming white and silver object that was shimmering its way towards the approach runway. Wssssnnnnnggggggsssshhhhhh. So quiet. So discreet. The customs officials were arguing about who would get to board this elegant, borrowed space-mobile, out of which stumbled a group of renegades: assorted comics, movie stars and rockers, all stiff from a night in a flying frat-house. The fragrant but squashed leis they'd accumulated during a fuel-stop in Hawaii were unceremoniously wrenched from their necks by bug-wary customs officials.

"You'll get nicer ones here," they smiled reassuringly.

The less bleary-eyed passengers noticed me first.

"Oh hello, Matron!" That's my nickname.

"Welcome! Good to see you. What . . . are you wearing wool?"

My favourite rock star pal had arrived in a tweed coat and beret.

"Get that stuff off before you pass out with heat exhaustion!"

The birthday boy emerged, shaggy, crumpled and congenial.

"He thinks he looks like Bono. Hello, Pamsy!"

Being a non-passenger I was prevented from running to kiss him by a smiling Fijian policeman in a smart black, gold and red jacket with a white zigzag-edged *sulu* and sandals. Someone pointed out the obvious:

"Anyone else noticed that everywhere Matron takes us, the menfolk wear skirts?"

"They're called *sulus* here," I replied. "And every one of you was seriously cute in a kilt."

The customs hall soon became a jam-session, as guitars, banjos, ukuleles were unpacked, poked and plonked.

An awestruck janitor approached another guest, giant black tattooed hand outstretched.

"Good Morning Vietnam!" he welcomed him proudly with a beautiful gold and white grin.

"Everyone on the bus!" I herded them to an ancient tour-mobile that bounced its way out of the airport, past roadside fruit stalls, suburban tropical gardens and bright purple bungalows. Men and children in shorts and T-shirts, carrying fish, firewood and bananas, stared curiously at us for a moment, then waved enthusiastically. We seemed a bit of a novelty, and not just because the tourist industry in Fiji took a bit of a dive after the 1999 coup. We passed a school where scores of barefoot teenagers played a muddy game of rugby, while schoolgirls watched demurely from the shade of a banyan tree. This is not a land of equal-opportunity contact sport.

After we turned on to a rough dirt road leading to dense jungle, some of our newcomers seemed uneasy, especially when we hit a deep pothole that sent them bouncing off the roof. They glanced at me with eyebrows raised. The waiting launch with its high mast ferried us dangerously close to over-river power lines. It wound through heron-filled mangrove swamps and miniature villages flanked by fishermen, eventually thrusting its way towards a vast sea-lagoon. In the far distance we could see the pearl-topped ridges of outer-reef breakers, and a landform to our left that resembled a gaping, green lizard.

Our island lay ahead, just inside the reef, enticingly wrapped in dense, dancing palms and scarves of ochre sand. A small pontoon awaited the first guests, some of whom were beginning to show signs of succumbing to jetlag. Having already banned laptops and hair-dryers, I divested everyone of the last overt trappings of a stressful, hi-tech lifestyle.

"Watches off, everybody!" I insisted. "No need to tell the time here . . . they'll beat the drum at meal times."

". . . and when I need to take my Zanax?" someone enquired.

"This whole place is one big Zanax," I replied. "You'll be destressed in no time."

A small crowd of *sulu*-clad Fijian people were waiting on the beach, singing a welcoming song, accompanied by battered guitars. This touristy scene, though engaging, was at odds with my original plan. I had hoped to recreate the experience of the first Caucasian contact with Fijian people, a historical scene that had long intrigued me. Of course I was thinking of early encounters that had positive outcomes, for if you were shipwrecked near Fiji at the beginning of the nineteenth century you were liable to be eaten. I had arranged for seven traditional outrigger canoes to be carved by local woodworkers especially for this celebration. As guests were paddled ashore by fierce-looking, painted, grass-skirted warriors with leafy amulets and anklets, they were greeted warmly with the word "*Bula*" and led to a shady seat. Nearby, a small palm bore a plaque that commemorated our wedding of 1989. Our name was misspelled.

Fijian society is steeped in ritual, and none could escape the official welcome. The kava or *Yaqona* ceremony is an important Fijian custom, without which we could not begin our sojourn on the island. Its meaning involves prestige and a symbolic affirmation of the chiefly system. People who buy manufactured "kava-kava" capsules in chemists' shops as an anti-anxiety supplement are usually unaware of the ceremony and importance of the drug in South Pacific culture. Made from a root, it was originally a chief's drink, untouched by common people, but now it is ubiquitous, especially among contemporary Fijian males. As we took our places in a semi-circle facing the seated Fijian group, our chatter died to a respectful silence, for the kava maker and master of ceremonies were fully focused on their solemn task. They sat cross-legged in T-shirts and brightly coloured *sulus* beside a large, polished wooden bowl (*tanoa*) containing a murky, grey-brown liquid. The cup-bearer, identified as a chief by the impressive boar's tooth hanging from his neck, held a half-coconut shell at the ready, but it would be a while before the first offering would be made. As one man languidly stirred the

221

mixture there were speeches and mysterious invocations, all in the Fijian language.

One of the first Europeans ever to participate in this ceremony was an early settler, or "beachcomber" as such people were known, called John Danford, who was asked to officiate at a kava ceremony by calling on the gods. By plagiarising characters from *The Arabian Nights* he convinced local people he knew the names of more gods than they did, thereby earning himself two fat pigs.

As we sat awkwardly on woven raffia mats, I noticed that those in my little group were avoiding eye-contact with each other for fear of breaking into nervous giggles. Eye-contact was absent among the Fijians too, but for a different reason; for in that particular society, politeness excludes it. There was an abundance of handclapping and chanting as the kava maker carefully strained the thin soup through a sodden rag. In earlier times the kava root was first chewed by the chiefs' favourite virgins, but here a good old pounding with a heavy stone sufficed. Eventually, the first direct address began, probably a speech of welcome for us. A visitors' reply is inappropriate in Fiji. Instead, Micah was nominated to articulate our thoughts, though his response was both intriguing and indecipherable. We searched in vain for meaning in gesture or facial expression, but all of these were absent in his flat, halting delivery. He must have got it right, however, for his prose was greeted by nods and grunts of approval. I was tugging at Billy's shirt to halt his natural inclination to join in with his own speech of appreciation. I'd

222

forgotten to warn him that it would not be culturally appropriate, but in the end he was encouraged by Micah to say his piece anyway.

"Thank you for welcoming us here," he said, sounding like an early beachcomber meeting a benign war-chief. Beachcombers first arrived in the South Pacific in the late eighteenth century. They were renegade settlers who had either jumped ship or been shipwrecked, or perhaps had tried to earn their living as pearl fishermen. When Christian missionaries arrived in the 1830s, they found beachcombers living among local people on most islands, using their firearms and blacksmithing skills, or their knowledge of European culture and language to maintain favour with the chiefs. They were rarely on good terms with missionaries, but the beachcombers had a perception and appreciation for island culture that was completely missed by other Europeans. Many of them succumbed to ritual tattooing to show loyalty to patron chiefs, and some married local women. Unfortunately, they were almost completely annihilated during inter-island and tribal wars.

As powerful and interesting as the kava ceremony was, it was nevertheless an unlikely situation to share with some of the world's "windswept and interesting". I felt close to giggling myself at times, and dared not look in the direction of some of our more irreverent guests, especially when it was my turn to clap my hands, take a gulp of the sour, tingly liquid, then clap again three times afterwards. Billy and I both took some small sadistic pleasure in observing the controlled expressions of those guests who had never tried it before. It was a bit like an episode of *Fear Factor*.

I am endlessly drawn to the South Pacific. I love the balmy climate, and the sea-breezes, the astonishingly beautiful, palm-lined beaches and the pure cornflower sky. I feel blessed by the scent of frangipani, the daily unfurling of hibiscus, and the way my body and mind uncurl to a peaceful, creative repose whenever I let go of time, as one does with impunity in places where it is utterly unimportant. I feel at home in the warm, buoyant sea with the creatures that live therein. Most of all, I love the people; their sweetness, their levity, and their unfathomable wisdom.

My mother was born in Fiji, and my grandmother spoke nostalgically of her days educating girls in a Methodist hostel in Suva. I sometimes think it would be nice to spend all my time in such an unpressured atmosphere, but that of course is fantasy. I recently came across a letter written by one of the early travellers that put me straight:

> Here, I at first thought my dreams of island felicity were to be realised . . . this could not continue. The gloss of novelty wore off in a few weeks, and disclosed the bareness and poverty of savage life, even in its most inviting forms. I grew wary of lying all day long in the shade, or lounging on the mats of a great house, or bathing in the bright waters. I soon found the quietude of life was but apparent. Petty feuds and open hostilities disturbed the small world.

My near-namesake Robert Louis Stevenson spent a portion of his life in nearby Samoa, and I was very drawn to visit it myself. Professionally, I was particularly interested in the group of male-bodied people with female attributes I've already mentioned known as *fa'afafine*. People with malleable gender have probably existed in the South Pacific for a very long time. In Hawaii, for example, the *mahu* are similar to the *fa'afafine* and there are early accounts of a favourite trick they played, presenting as real women for the benefit of horny heterosexual seafarers, who were horrified by their eventual discoveries.

The night sky is particularly radiant in the South Pacific. It was lovely to lie out on the porch in the early evening and gaze at my childhood watch star, the Southern Cross, with its low, extra-brilliant pointer. Even the Milky Way seems to glow more vibrantly in that part of the world. It was just as well, for one needed to keep an eye on the ground to avoid the sleepy, black and golden striped sea snakes called *dadakulaci* that slither ashore from time to time. Their venom is deep in their throats and their tiny jaws cannot bite humans, but some people hyperventilate when they spot them, as evidenced by sporadic shrieks emanating from various parts of the island. It is a natural human urge to seek and destroy anything that seems so threatening, but the beautiful creatures are sacred to the local people and must never be harmed.

Kava has a tendency to stop one's legs from working. Fortunately no one quite got to that stage, and we bravely made our way to our separate *bures*. The guests slid off their shoes and bathed their jet-swollen feet in giant clam-shell baths before entering the thatched-palm bedrooms. Inside, lofty gecko-decked ceilings held ceiling-fans supported by rope-lashed cross-beams. Intricately woven wall-coverings contrasted with simple cotton-covered beds adjacent to bamboo furniture laden with striking tropical flowers and fruit. We all soaked ourselves in warm water and coconut soap, before passing out to the soothing timpani of gentle, steamy rain.

Next day, I walked along the beach to find a fallen night-flower. There is a tree on this island where each bud blossoms for just one night into a giant and voluptuous pale pinky-violet bloom with scores of long, sweet stamens protruding from its centre. After blossoming fully throughout the night, each fragile flower falls to the sand. You can pick one up, ever so gently lest it disintegrate, and continue your walk while taking deep breaths of its intoxicating scent.

Before long, the sonorous beating of hollow wood led us all to fresh banana muffins, papaya and tea, after which I approached the birthday boy.

"Some of us are going to learn to scuba. We'll take a lesson in the pool today, then go out to the reef tomorrow. Wanna join us?"

Miraculously, Billy had managed to get himself into a hammock without hitting the sand. He was reading *Half Asleep in Frog Pajamas*, which title seemed to suit his state of consciousness.

"No thanks," he said with a yawn. "Not me."

226

I was not surprised. Being a poor swimmer, an uncomfortable sailor, and shark-shy in the extreme, it seemed best to let him be. Unfortunately, there are times when I just can't help myself.

"Come on," I said. "I bet you'll be sorry if you don't."

He paused for a minute, then dangled one leg outside its ropey holder.

"I've always thought it would be such a lovely thing to do," he said wistfully, "but I'm not much good in the water. I don't know how I'd get on."

"Well," I said, "if you want to try it, I could arrange a private lesson for you, so you won't have to worry about other people. If you don't like it in the pool there's no need to continue."

An hour later I wandered past the swimming pool and saw a black shape sitting at the bottom of the deep end, blowing bubbles. A familiar shock of grey hair floated out of an orange mask. He looked utterly happy.

"That was brilliant!" he cried once he surfaced. "I'm ready for the reef! I can take my mask off underwater and everything!"

"You're going tomorrow," I said firmly. "Just the three of us who've done it before are going this afternoon because it's very choppy out there."

Billy vomits in dinghies. There's just no other way to put it.

There certainly was a sizable swell. As we bounced towards the site of a nineteenth-century shipwreck I wondered if we'd ever drop anchor.

"I guess we'll be OK if the boat capsizes." I grimaced at Rachel, our dive guide. "We're fully prepared for submersion."

It was calmer beneath the waves. Sunlight radiated through the coral gardens, even at twelve metres. I was intrigued to see one of the black-banded sea snakes I'd met on land swimming vertically like a cork-screw at ten metres. It was peering into crevices for something tasty. Brilliant blue-striped fish fed among giant anemones, while regal angel fish and golden sea-butterflies snapped up succulent polyps. We followed Rachel through a narrow chasm between two gigantic columns, rich with flame-coloured sea fans, creamy brain coral, and magenta acroporid. I kept a wary look-out for snapping Moray eels that lay in wait in murky fissures. Land aquariums I'd visited with the children had accentuated the downside of a chance encounter with one of those repulsive sea-reptiles. The canyon formed a fishy freeway and wound through an underwater rush hour of fast-changing lanes of darting silver baby fish and show-off black-finned cruisers. We marvelled at huge purple star fish and zebra-striped spider shells, and even spotted a pristine white cowrie shell.

Eventually the passageway opened out on to an underwater graveyard, the resting place of a massive sailing ship. Huge rusty chains, steering wheel sections and part of the ship's anchor had become living sculptures in fishy playgrounds. My companion found a couple of comic props: a sea-cucumber straight off Ann Summers's shelf and a pointy thing with beady eyes. I

228

was delighted to discover one could howl with laughter even underwater.

We traced the lines of the vessel's dark orange skeleton, delicately adorned with turtle grass, crimson feather stars and rare sea lilies, and thought of the souls who had perished here. Eventually, our surroundings seemed to become brighter, and I realised we had been ascending. I glanced at Rachel to make sure we were within our nitrogen limits, and she gave me the thumbs up. Before us now was a vast plain with a faraway sandy bottom. Several large, fat stripy fish with huge, saucer eyes approached us. They were so amusing they looked like they'd been drawn and animated by Walt Disney, yet their demeanour was somehow threatening. I saw Rachel pointing far below to extensive circles in the sand and backing away. I did not know at the time, but they belonged to the trigger fish beside us, truly aggressive creatures despite their appearance. They will shoot darts at anything that ventures within the conical boundaries of their sandy nests, and we had perilously encroached upon their territory.

As we swam on, and I was just telling myself that I had never before experienced such glorious natural beauty. I suddenly saw our first shark. Although it was far below us, my heart rate doubled in an instant. My instinct was to do the sensible thing and move sideways towards a coral shelf, but Rachel motioned us on with great excitement, pointing to three or four more of the grey reef monsters ahead, all thankfully in bottom-feeding mode.

"They're not interested in us." I repeated Rachel's earlier words to myself like a mantra, but found myself using up oxygen at a terrifying rate.

"I wish I'd seen them!" cried Billy when we got back to the island.

"Well, perhaps you will tomorrow," I threatened.

I half-expected Billy to bail out of his first reef dive, but there he was on the jetty waiting for the dive boat, happily riffing on the subject of peeing in a wet suit. It perhaps wasn't the best subject for this moment, and I could see that his fellow divers seemed unsure about his joining them.

"That would definitely attract sharks," cautioned one. "You might wanna go do potty before we leave."

Billy shrugged disarmingly and climbed aboard with Danny and Rachel. He waved goodbye to me and I watched them buffeting their way across outer-reef choppiness.

Billy under the water proved to be exactly the same as Billy on land: a human windmill, apt to startle or shock with never a hint of warning. He made it out to the dive site without barfing in the boat, which was a huge achievement for him. But then, after descending without incident for eleven metres, his weight belt suddenly shot off and sank to the bottom, causing Billy to fly up towards the surface like a rescue-flare. Immediately grasping the dangerousness of the situation, Rachel bolted after him and tried to pull him down. This she managed about as effectively as a kitten trying to contain a bear. Although Billy was way too heavy for her, she managed to drag him sideways to a coral outgrowth and indicated that he should literally hang on for dear life.

"Ah'd seen a bunch of *Sea Hunt* episodes." Danny told us afterwards, his southern accent adding more to the humour of the situation rather than to the dramatic tension. "Ah'd always wanted to be Lloyd Bridges, so Ah decided to go after that belt. Ah found it, but it was too heavy for me to lift. Ah thought to myself, 'Where the hell's Lloyd now we really need him?' "

Danny eventually managed to drag the fallen object up to its owner, who had meantime lost so much oxygen trying to hang on to the coral he was now buddy-breathing with Rachel.

"When Ah got to him, his legs were flying straight up in the air," reported Danny. "But Rachel had a hold of him, like a little critter guarding a whole winter carcass."

Once stabilised, they crept back to the surface. I was shaken when I heard the story.

"I made him go, you know," I confessed to the group, but no one believed me. Far from being distressed by his watery adventure, Billy himself was thrilled. He completely ignored the fact that he'd just had a near-death experience and focused on his observations of life at thirty-six feet beneath the surface.

"Everything that grows under the sea looks like a penis or a vagina," he mused. "Actually, being down in the depths is like swimming through a gigantic sex act. I think the sea is just one big fucking-organ." The experience had, however, confirmed his earlier belief that humans don't belong in the ocean.

"Everywhere you turn there's something to make you feel uncomfortable," he complained. "It's the primordial ooze. All the time, you're getting a big fucking hint that you're not welcome there. Even if you see something ordinary, like a boulder for example, there'll be a massive abyss on the other side. If you see something shadowy you can bet your arse something's hiding in there. Something weird."

"What did it feel like," I asked gingerly. "when you lost your belt? You could have got the bends."

"It didn't bother me," he replied. "At those times when other people are inspired to yell 'Help!' at the top of their voices I go, 'This is interesting.' It's not a healthy thing, and hardly courage, but more a complex kind of stupidity. Any time I've been in a position of extreme danger, like heading for another vehicle sideways, or falling from a ship into the Clyde when I was a welder, or being in a faulty parachute it was the same. When my helmet hit the fuselage of the aeroplane, I didn't go, 'Fucking hell! I just hit the plane!' . . . I went, 'This is interesting. This is what the death knell's like.' "

It was a privilege to be able to hang out with the local people on the island. We danced together, played volley ball together and played music together every evening. Fijians in general are extremely musical people, and their beautiful voices and tuneful harmonising impressed us all. I was proud of my friends. When Zac, a young guitarist whose job it was to serenade visitors, confessed he lacked an instrument of his own, there was a whip round and a trip into Suva to purchase one for him. We were treated to a melodious choir practice most evenings, in preparation for Sunday's cross-cultural service that combined hymn-singing, sermon, prayers and kava. Men who attended it wore dark jackets, collars and ties . . . with *sulus* and bare feet.

We visited neighbouring island villages to drink cups of tea and eat cake with smiling elders and children. We had picnics on uninhabited islands, rich with red-footed pale boobies with black-tipped wings, bright-throated lesser frigates, guano and stripy, second-hand snakeskin. We net-fished, raced canoes, and played island-rules boules in the sand, and reef golf when the tide went out. Mostly we laughed. It was heaven.

I had arranged for a Fijian contemporary dance group from the university to perform for us before our final dinner. When the dancers disembarked from their launch I was particularly struck by their choreographer, a tall, beautiful Samoan person with striking gender ambivalence, whose name, I learned, was Allan. I decided to approach him privately.

"I understand you are from Samoa?" I asked.

"Yes," replied Allan, golden earrings twinkling on both ears.

"May I ask . . ." I was praying my question would not be offensive, "are you by any chance *fa'afafine?*"

"Honey," replied Allan in perfect English, eyes lighting up, "I'm a twenty-four-hours-a-day, card-carrying *fa'afafine!*"

"I'm dying to talk to you," I said, terribly excited. Later, I sat down in private with him (or, more accurately, her although it turned out that the pronouns are used interchangeably in Samoa because their experience of gender is malleable). "What does it mean to you to be *fa'afafine?*"

"It's funny, because I feel male yet female. I feel like I am both, and that I was born to be both. I have the strength of a male, and a spirit of a female." I noticed Allan had a remarkable tattoo that seemed to cover every inch of skin from waist to knee.

"It must be unusual," I remarked, "for a *fa'afafine* to have a *pe'a.*" That is a ritual tattoo, known as a symbol of maleness and high status.

Allan told me an extraordinary tale. In common with transgendered people all over the world, he had undergone excruciating pain. In his case, this was in the form of being tattooed in the traditional manner (with a shark's tooth and without any anaesthetic), in order to prove to his disparaging father that he was manly. After it was finished he did gain the respect of his father, and was finally allowed to say "I love you". I was terribly moved by his story, and longed to learn more about what it was like for other *fa'afafine*. I was thrilled when Allan said he would accompany me to Samoa the following January and introduce me to the *fa'afafine* community.

234

When I told Billy just a little about Allan, he too was filled with admiration for him. Billy loves brave people of all kinds. He was particularly taken with a man he saw wearing twinset and pearls outside a gay pub in London singing "I Wanna Be Bobby's Girl". Billy loves Robert, his homeless friend with schizophrenia who lives in the alley behind a coffee shop on Ventura Boulevard, and especially loves people who scream at inanimate objects, such as the ones who trip in the street and shout, "That should have been fixed fucking years ago!"

Our last evening on the island was Billy's true birthday.

"Finally!" he sighed with relief. "Soon it'll be a thing of the past."

I didn't want to tell him we'd be crossing the dateline on the way home, and that he'd have yet another birthday in a few hours. Better keep that one to myself. Just before we left, Billy was presented with a *Tabua*, a symbolic whale's tooth that signified his honoured status, while Vern, a jolly New Zealander who owns the island, gave Billy a teddy bear whose eyes had been focused inwards.

"His name is Gladly," he announced. "Remember?"

Billy had long ago spoken on stage about his misinterpretation of the well-known hymn that contains the words "Gladly the cross I'd bear". Billy had sung another version his entire childhood: "Gladly, the cross-eyed bear". His mistake always resonated with me, since for my entire childhood I had sung the first line of the Australian National Anthem that goes

"Australia's Sons, Let us rejoice" in my own mistaken form that went: "Australia's sunset ostriches".

That night the whole gang ate local fish, ferns and seaweed by candlelight, with a backdrop of phosphorus-tinged seas. It was a touching evening. Each of us spoke from the heart about our time on the island, the rare moments of connection and camaraderie we'd managed to grab despite our hectic lives, and our sadness at having to leave it all the next day. Tears flowed, and there was a sense that we'd been blessed to get in touch with something all too elusive in our own society. Then Billy was treated to a fantastic surprise: a guest who had earned the name "Crispy White Boy" due to his shocking sunburn, sang a song he composed especially called "The Hairy Banjo", with a stunning chorus of local Fijian people who are singing it to this day. It was a perfect finale.

Just after Tonga on the way home, Billy reverted to fifty-nine, then immediately turned sixty all over again when the new dawn broke. "Happy Birthday to you!" everyone began again.

"Fucking give it a rest," he implored.

Back in Los Angeles, the flipping of channels on American Thanksgiving Day provided a bizarre contrast of feast and fear: the unlikely image of *Breakfast Club* star Molly Ringwold belting out "Cabaret" with a background of the Brooklyn Bridge; a gigantic inflatable Ronald McDonald in Superman flying pose soaring above the Rockefeller Center; an

236

inflatable retroville Jimmy Neutron, all twelve thousand cubic feet of it. Five thousand dancers shivered in lime green and peach spandex, while pom-pom squads pirouetted beneath a Happy the Hippo novelty balloon that weighed five tons.

On another channel it was a "day of terror" as shaken passengers exited their Tel Aviv flight after escaping two missile attempts. Two launch tubes were recovered from a nearby field. The heat-seeking stinger has a range of eleven thousand feet, said the reporter.

"How lucky do you feel?" I asked Billy who would be flying to Africa after Christmas. There had just been three suicide bombers and bloody scenes at the Mombasa Hotel. Live from Crawford, Texas, the White House condemned the attacks but no one knew who to blame. Maybe a bunch of vengeful turkeys. As I sat morosely contemplating this mess, a CNN poll was introduced.

What do you think? Should all passenger planes be protected by anti-missile artillery, irrespective of the extra cost? Check Yes or No.

Duh!

Billy was entirely oblivious to all this. He was rushing round the house preparing to leave for an appointment with his chiropractor.

"Cheerio," he said. "I'm away to get my arse felt."

CHAPTER
ELEVEN

Christmas Eve And Still No Offer Of Panto

December 25th, 1947 was not too different from other days in the Connolly tenement flat. In Billy's five-year-old experience Christmas was pretty much just something that happened at church with the singing of carols and a change of priestly vestments. Sometimes there would be a swaddled rag doll lying in a wood-and-straw manger with a cardboard angel standing guard. Paper decorations livened up the windows in a few shops in well-to-do areas, but tinsel was scarce in these parts. In those times, Christmas Day was not considered a holiday for many working class people. The adults in the household, Billy's father and two aunts, all went to their jobs, so the family did not sit down to Christmas dinner. As usual, Billy's father thrust himself grumpily out of the door at 8a.m. to catch the bus to his job at the Singer machine factory.

238

The previous day, Christmas Eve, Billy had looked forward to pub closing time, when his father would come home from work and hand him a pillow case to hang at the end of his bed. When he awoke he made an unceremonious dive for it. The first items his fingers felt inside were some sweeties and an orange. Further down were a few toys, a rubber ball and a pocket handkerchief. Best of all, there was a harmonica, a piercing music-maker that could double as an ear-splitter.

As soon as Billy was dressed, in grey flannel shorts and a pale blue shirt, he ran helter-skelter down to the street to see which of his little pals might be about. Standing outside his tenement building, he gazed up and down Stewartville Street, but the freezing pavement was virtually empty. Only Gerald Magee, his friend from the ground-floor flat, was busy bouncing a shiny new ball against the wall of the close.

"Eh, Billy," Gerald stashed the ball under one arm and waved him over with the other. "C'mere! I want to show you something!" He charged off in great excitement, and ran ahead to the door of his flat. Billy followed warily. He had learned from experience that Gerald was well capable of leading him on a wild goose chase. Not that Billy minded a prank or a bit of mischief, but today of all days he was hoping to avoid a walloping when his father got home.

As they approached Gerald's flat, Billy could hear high-spirited conversation and happy laughter emanating from within. "There must be a dozen people inside," he thought. "I wonder what that din is all

239

about." It never occurred to him that it might be a family Christmas gathering, for the Connollys did not engage in such a joyful rite. Gerald paused mysteriously at his front door, like a magician about to perform the finale of his best illusion, then prodded it open with a flourish.

"Look at that!" he said, proudly.

Inside, there was as much of a festive wonderland as Billy had ever seen. A straggly Scottish pine had been dragged in from the outer suburbs, and was sitting gaily in a plastic tub. Gerald's mother and grandmother had covered it with coloured paper chains and tinsel, and, most gloriously of all, there were several large red, silver and gold balls dancing precariously on its branches. Hoping he wouldn't be shooed away by the merry-making adults, tipsy on cheap whisky even though the hour was early, Billy crept closer till he could peer at his own face, miraculously distorted in a silver globe.

"God," he thought. "What a thing to have in your house!"

As Billy grew older, he noticed that signs of Christmas became more visible in the neighbourhood. His primary school, St Peter's, was never decorated, but his family eventually began to get a tree, hung with "jingle balls" as his cousin Mike would call them. He was mystified, though, by the repetitious nature of the gifts he received. Harmonicas, for example: he seemed to get one year after year. Not so welcome was the annual Conway Stewart pen set, a fountain pen accompanied by either a ballpoint or propelling pencil, nestling side by side on midnight taffeta in a cardboard presentation box. That set was a bugger of a thing to look after. By the time February came around he'd either have lost it, or else some bastard at school would have stolen it. Billy would end up with a thrashing for carelessness.

Billy still loves Christmas trees. Jingle balls continue to be his favourite decoration, but he is also fond of the painted wooden cowboy boots we hang every year, the Indian mirror balls, and the tree lights made of fishing sinkers. Most of all he adores those decorations our children have made through the years: laminated, ribbon-hung pictures, papier mâché bells and torn but treasured paper chains. Apart from their prettiness, Christmas trees seem to have provided him with a yardstick of his career achievement from season to season. The first year he began to be nationally successful, his children James and Cara had a tree each.

"What's happened to me?" He was overawed by the sheer extravagance of it all.

As Christmas 2002 approached, Alan, a brave and nimble soul who tends the Candacraig gardens, shinned up the huge sequoia by the forecourt and clothed it with enough lights to illuminate the clouds.

Billy was worried we'd wipe out the power in the entire neighbourhood with such a display, but it lit our way as we clowned around after dark on spiffing wooden toboggans I'd bought from a catalogue. Billy, wrapped in a tartan blanket coat and feathered cowboy hat, shook his head disapprovingly.

"You'd be better off on tea trays," he grumbled.

Billy can only take so much of the holiday spirit. With only four days to go before Christmas, he began to show signs of incurable bahhumbugness. He escaped to London with my blessing.

"I'm nipping down to visit Jeffrey Archer in prison," he explained, then added as if he needed another excuse: "Jeffrey's always been very hospitable to me . . ."

It was true. Shepherd's pie parties and an eclectic human menu. Jeffrey's new home seemed more factory than jail. As Billy sauntered in, an officer confiscated his Licorice Allsorts. He supposed they could have been drugs or weapons. "You never know," he said, "someone might invent the Smartie bomb." He waited moodily at a plastic-topped table in a spartan meeting-hall until Jeffrey appeared wearing jeans and a blue, stripy shirt. They joined the cafeteria line.

"It's nice to get a turkey sandwich." Jeffrey seemed cheerful.

Billy presented him with *Samuel Pepys, Life of Pi* and *Rumpole of the Bailey.*

"To take you back to your old court case and warm the cockles of your heart," he grinned.

"What a beautiful selection!" Jeffrey was delighted. "If I could have walked into a bookshop I would have picked those up myself!"

"What's it like in here?" asked Billy.

"The humour's good," he said. "One man in here told another to 'get a life', and he replied, 'I've already got two . . . how many would you like me to have?'"

The two men gossiped for a while before Billy's insatiable curiosity got the better of him.

"Now you've been shagged on a regular basis by Mexican transvestites," said Billy, "you'll have changed your political views, I hope?"

Billy's visit with Jeffrey had provided just the right degree of appreciation for his considerable blessings. By Christmas Eve, he had became less Grinch and more Santa Claus impersonator, wandering around in a woolly hat that Scarlett had knitted him, a T-shirt with "Bollocks" written on it after the style of Glaswegian artist Mackintosh (or Mockintosh as it's known), tweed tartan knee breeches and multi-coloured hose with individual toe-pouches.

"I love you, Dad, you're such a freak," said Amy.

All family presents had to be hand-made this year. That was my rule. Billy had intended to write everyone a song but had failed to do so. He ended up with the usual Christmas Eve bum's-rush in the form of a fifteen-minute splurge at Heathrow airport.

"What was your favourite present?" I asked as we lolled in front of the fire.

"The Hardy's Collectors fishing reels." That had been my cheat gift. Hardly hand-made, but I couldn't resist. They were a long way from his first telescopic ex-army rod but Billy thinks they are stunning, and loves the metallic *wheee!* they make as the fish takes off. They are supposed to be put away and kept in mint condition, but Billy said he planned to use them. He abhors the hoarding of lovely, usable things, especially guitars, banjos and mandolins.

"They put 'em on walls and stop those wonderful instruments being used," he says. "Bastards!"

On Boxing Day Billy and James took off for Celtic Park in Glasgow to watch his team play Hearts (short for "Heart of Midlothian", the Sir Walter Scott novel). Their maroon-clad supporters are known as Jam Tarts, or Jambos. I had not known that until he told me; in fact I am remarkably ignorant about football. We recently passed a Celtic FC merchandising shop in Glasgow and I noticed there was a green-and-white team jersey in the window with the word Carling written across the front.

"I didn't know Will Carling played for Celtic," I innocently remarked. I'll leave Billy's retort to your imagination.

While Billy and James attended the Celtic-Hearts game, the rest of us rose late, took a long, wet, chilly walk then back to hot soup and a fireside game of Boggle. When Billy returned, I caught him in the middle of his victory dance.

"Don't suppose you won, then?" I teased him.

"Beautiful! Dainty. Very light, short passing in the middle of all those muscles and sweat and grunting. It was a joy, an absolute joy to see."

"Have you been watching football or a porn flick?" I asked.

Five days later, Billy, licorice smuggler, jingle-ball lover and jam tart watcher, sat petrified in a seven-seater Soviet plane bound for Somaliland, bursting for a piss.

"Another hour, eh?" He winced at Dave, the ex-military man beside him.

"We'll be in Hargeisa in two hours forty-three exactly," hollered Dave, above the raucous spluttering of ancient propellers. "Care for some water?"

"Fuck, no. My back teeth are afloat."

Nearly three hours. He sighed. Purgatory at twelve thousand feet. Billy began to scan the aircraft interior for an emergency receptacle. Nothing in sight. At a pinch, he could finish Dave's water then use the bottle . . . nah . . . given the size of its neck he'd have about as much chance of getting his aim right as landing the plane himself. He peered through his insect-caked window, and grimly noted an approaching cloud bank. Wasn't monsoon season over? There was also the issue of women on board. There were two of them, BBC film crew and Comic Relief workers, who might easily take exception to the sight of a celebrity Scotsman weeing ineptly into a bottle — even if they had already seen his penis on TV, flapping happily round Piccadilly Circus in broad daylight. Now, in this situation, would a willy-sighting be tantamount to criminal flashing?

"I'm an ex-para man," he reminded himself. "I know how to make a jump. I could just ask for a wee parachute . . ."

In any case, that might be the safest option. Just before take-off, the pilot had taken them through the emergency drill.

"There's an exit on either side of the aircraft," he'd instructed. "Life-rafts are under your seats, and the door handles work like so . . ." At this point the passengers' attention was drawn to a plaque tacked above one of the exits: *Fear not: your God is with you.* The group had fallen uncomfortably silent. "It's all very well," he'd thought, "trying to help hungry Africans, but did a chap really have to risk his arse?"

"And before we go," continued the young pilot, "we'll just have a little prayer."

"Prayer!" said Billy. "I'd rather he was poring over his flying-school manual. Bollocks to praying, do a bit of swotting."

They took off into dust-cloud. Beneath them lay the Somali coastline, a great gig for pirates, kidnappers and terrorists.

At exactly the same moment in time, the children and I were gathered in front of our television back in Los Angeles to watch the American Superbowl half-time show. The country cross-over star Shania Twain was strutting around the cakewalk in an outrageous, futuristic outfit, with sequinned bra and "Trekkie" cape. The family TV room was a wreck; the customary lime chilli chips, salsa and avocado dip had been depleted, the barbecue was nearing its usual, over-cooked state, and half-drunk cans of soft drink littered the coffee table. Uninterested in the game itself, they'd marvelled at the miracles of hydraulic set-changing that revealed Sting howling a solo, and critiqued the famous million-dollar Superbowl commercials: Willie Nelson assuaging his personal taxation embarrassment with an ad for the revenue people, Jack and Kelly Osbourne transmogrified into the Osmond duo for Pepsi, and Shaq being a golden god for the Nike company. We lapped it up. This was a family of well-fed, card-carrying consumers, if ever there was one.

"Guess what I'm doing?" Scarlett asked her sisters. She had an open copy of *Glamour* magazine on her knees, and was becoming brainwashed by the ads.

"What?" chorused Amy and Daisy.

"I'm cooling and reviving my tired eyes."

Our teenage children were oblivious to the inherent dangers in their father's African journey, but I had already stated my objections.

"Oh, pish," Billy had protested. "You watch too much CNN."

"It doesn't take a news junkie to figure out what's number one on their video charts . . ."

He had glared at me perplexedly.

"'. . . How to Operate an SA7 Shoulder-Fire Anti-Aircraft Missile'," I rounded.

"Shut up. I'm still going."

"Billy, this is too much to ask of you. Haven't you done enough for Comic Relief already? Raised millions of pounds? Shown your willy a billion times on BBC1?"

"No more naked stuff," he proclaimed. "Naked's finished. I think I took it to its logical conclusion at Piccadilly Circus. Actually I don't think I could take it much further . . . What would I do next?"

Well, there are a few possibilities, but I decided not to tempt fate by mentioning them.

Forty-one minutes to go. Billy frantically loosened his belt, undid the last fly button, and stretched his body into a shape that soothed his pulsing bladder as much as possible. He glanced out of the window. The terrain below had changed to desert. Shanty towns and bush punctuated a pale brown, arid landscape, but apart from that there was nothing. He closed his eyes and imagined being on the ground. Africa has a smell he really likes. A slightly perfumey, dry smell, of desert and dancing bodies. Billy says you can only recognise it if you've been there. When you smell it again, it's a sign that you're back.

Mind over matter can only go so far. Billy's discomfort was intensifying beyond the bearable, and he knew that drastic action was necessary. He glanced around at his fellow passengers. No one looked entirely comfortable; perhaps he was not the only one with a burning bladder. He unclicked his safety belt and stretched forward to alert the pilot he was about to explode. Krrrraaccckkkk! A sudden, hideously sharp grinding movement caused his adrenalin to surge. The plane pitched alarmingly then began to shudder. The lower half of his body began bouncing at a faster pace than the rest and he grappled unsuccessfully for something solid to hang on to.

"I'm going to die two ways at once," he decided. "Plane going down like a burning Spitfire, with wee bits of my bladder all over the cockpit."

The shuddering increased to roller-coaster pitch, before the plane banked steeply and entered a kamikaze dive. He pressed both hands on his groin to try to alleviate the pressure, but was being thrown sideways too aggressively to be able to maintain it.

"Fasten your seatbelt!" the pilot yelled at him, and six pairs of hands made a simultaneous grab to steady him, just before the plane hit the tarmac. Flags, cameras, dignitaries, all flashed by his window to the music of yelping brakes, yet it barely registered that he was safely on the ground. As the aircraft doors were wrenched open, the Health Minister's welcoming committee approached with gifts in hand. They froze, open-mouthed, as their Very Important Guest flew inelegantly past their outstretched arms, his open fly and denim arse a mere blur on his way to the terminal's comfort zone.

"I'll take that as a sign that I'd better start paying attention," Billy told the cracked mirror in the Hargeisa International Airport urinal. "All that birthday shite. It's time to own up."

They reached the township of Hargeisa before nightfall, past a plain of crimson bush. There was just enough twilight to look around the place, but there wasn't that much to see. Brown women swathed in vibrant, patterned scarves bore bags on their heads and babies on their backs. Children crowded around him, smelling delightfully like wood smoke and campfires. In this media-thin place, Billy's hairiness drew far more attention than his celebrity. Everywhere Billy went, children patted his arm and rubbed their faces on him, as though he was a dog. "Ahhh!" they sang, and touched his beard.

"I like being patted," Billy informed me. "It's very pleasant."

Something always draws him back to Africa, and it's not just his admiration of the people. In colonial days people spoke of a yearning for Africa they called Mal d'Afrique, and Billy has caught it badly. He hoped he would get to dance with the people. He loves doing that.

Somaliland is situated on the eastern horn of Africa, at the crossroads between Europe, the Middle East and South East Asia, and is about the size of England and Wales put together. It shares borders with the Republic of Djibouti to the west, the Federal Republic of Ethiopia to the south and Somalia to the east. The Somaliland Protectorate, as it was known, came under British rule from 1884 until it got its independence in 1960 and joined the former Italian Somalia to form the Somali Republic. The union did not work because the people didn't want it, and the strain led to a civil war from the 1980s onwards and eventually to its collapse.

Around three and a half million people live in Somaliland, and fifty-five per cent of them are either nomadic or semi-nomadic. The country has a tropical monsoon type of climate with four distinct seasons. Billy experienced part of the long dry winter from December to March when the temperatures are between fifteen to twenty-six degrees centigrade. It is the most difficult time for the animal herding rural population and the farmers. If the April-June rains fail, the resultant drought could kill most animals, which have already become greatly weakened by the December-March dry season. That in turn severely hits the country's economy. It's hard to understand why the fishing industry has not been developed, because Somaliland has a northern coastal line that extends nearly six hundred miles along the Red Sea. Most people eat meat, and the backbone of the economy is livestock. There are supposedly twenty-four million livestock in the country, but many people are hungry.

Hargeisa, the capital of the third-poorest country in the world, boasted a modest hotel, restaurant and a decrepit gas station. Billy left it all next day for a patchwork city on a putrid rubbish dump in the middle of a gold-scrub desert. It was an encampment of nomadic refugees, who dwell in igloo-shaped "benders" fashioned of sticks and rags. Over fifty per cent of the city had been displaced by war, then migrated back with nowhere to dwell. A gold-brown baby had just been born in his rubbish-tip tent. His mother handed him to Billy.

"Diddly Dee Mi Daddio," sang Billy, rocking him to a tune from his own culture.

"*You can come to see the baby any time you*
   care to call
He's lying beside his mammy in a wee white
   shawl.
He looks so beat and swanky like a dumpling in
   a hanky
And we're going to call him William Angus
   Jamieson Jock McCall."

"He's a beauty," clucked Billy, employing his special baby-calming technique. It's nothing in particular, just a warm, enveloping cuddle, but it always works. Billy says African babies don't cry much. They're always right next to their mother, on her back or over her shoulder. The woman had four or five other children, Billy couldn't tell. It was dark inside the bender and he couldn't make out the shapes. Each day, they explained, their father went out to try to find work, lifting objects and sweeping, whatever he could get. Billy thought it was the hardest life imaginable.

Out in another part of the desert, Billy was thrilled to meet a local man with vivid red dyed hair. Naturally, Billy bonded with him instantly. Jibreel is a qualified veterinarian, funded by Comic Relief to train other people in animal husbandry. Best of all, as far as Billy was concerned, he was also a musician. He played the *oudh*, a pear-shaped, ten-stringed instrument that is a bit like a mandolin, only larger. The two men sat together under the stars that night, strummed the *oudh* by a campfire and talked of many things.

Billy would never normally have thought to ask why a man had dyed his hair crimson, for as a fellow coif-colourer he assumed it was designed as an arsehole-detector. But during their conversation he learned that Jibreel's hair was red for a different reason. When his village came under attack from Somalian fighters, he and his family fled for their lives. They walked stealthily through night after night until they eventually reached Ethiopia. It was a terrifying journey, under threat of death from both humans and wild hyenas. When they were finally safe, Jibreel found that his hair had turned white from the terror of it all, so he dyed it blood-red as a statement of protest against the bloodiness of war and what it does to families like his.

The next day I was able to reach Billy by phone.

"How are you doing?" I had been worried, with him out of contact.

"Och, a wee bit tired. A bit overwhelmed. But, because I've been in Africa before, I was prepared for the dreadfulness of it. It's not the same shock as the first time I saw such things."

"Have you had anything to eat?"

"Mmm, you get beyond the meal thing. I'm not here to see how starving feels, I'm here to do a bit of good for these poor buggers. Anyway, I never eat much here. I'm too scared I'll get the shits and be unable to work."

As always, when Billy visits countries where the water is unsafe to drink, I was worried that his difficulty focusing would lead him to forget about the importance of drinking and cleaning his teeth in only bottled water. In the past, he has become extremely ill through his inattention.

"Risk is a subjective entity," says Dave, the security expert who accompanied Billy to Somaliland. A Scottish ex-Parachute Regiment man with a great deal of experience in his chosen field, he specialises in organisational risk, kidnap and ransom, and teaching journalists how to survive in hostile environments. Billy enjoyed his company, for they had a lot in common, and they spent a great deal of time together.

Dave is the second youngest of a family of five children that lived in a small Scottish mining village. His family was Protestant, but next door was a Catholic family with twenty-one children and next to them was another Catholic family with twelve children. Add to that nine more children among two more Protestant families across the road, and as you might imagine quite a team would form when it was time for a game of "kick the can".

"It was just like in Billy's street," says Dave. "An adult would go out and pick any five kids and feed them. There was a fine community spirit."

Dave joined the army, which seemed a better option than staying in his home town. His father had begun working in the local foundry at fourteen, but eventually contracted black lung and died of it. He had instilled a strong work ethic in Dave, who also had to care for his mother.

"Scotland is the universal centre for denial when it comes to alcoholism," says Dave. "I used to drive Mum to AA but she'd go in one door and out the other." People who take care of others for a living have often begun their work in their family of origin.

Billy had been in safe hands. Astoundingly savvy about the region, Dave had headed off a potentially lethal situation.

"We were driving back in a three-car convoy and I was in the front vehicle with Billy," said Dave. "There was a photographer in the rear. It was mid afternoon so all the local people were high on *qat*, the chewable amphetamine that is sold everywhere. A dazed man suddenly walked out on to the road, right in front of the first vehicle in the convoy. The cars frightened him, so he involuntarily hit the vehicle with a piece of wood.

The secret police, who followed the film crew at all times, turned up three seconds later and started whipping him with sticks. Billy naturally wanted to join the fracas and try to fight them off."

I gulped when he told me this story for, given my husband's volatility, I immediately knew how close they came to disaster. The driver of Billy's car had apparently said, "Oh look, that's the police beating him up!" Thankfully, Dave intervened.

"Keep driving," he commanded in a low voice, knowing he had to keep Billy right away from that Scenario. Dave took it upon himself to tell the police to quit their heavy-handedness, at least in sight of the crew.

"Over there, the police version of crowd control is to throw stones at people. They whip people at the old football ground on a regular basis. Just kids. Thousands turn up."

Billy's experience in the group of shacks known as the Hargeisa hospital was life-changing. Two local workers, with twenty-four children between them, have been working in the X-ray department for years without any protective equipment. The one sterilising unit had been left behind by the British in the 1950s. Billy watched doctors operating on a man who'd got his hand caught in a cement mixer. Their procedure involved cutting off his thumb with a pair of scissors. Patients lay on stained beds covered in flies, goats wandered through the wards, urinating on the floor. No one has any money, so people sell everything they have to buy a child some treatment. Wild animals, syringes and torn bags of razor blades were scattered around the grounds, along with scrunched-up empty packs of *qat*. The leaf of the *qat* bush is apparently one of the few stimulants sanctioned by Islam. It is said that in nearby Somalia at the height of the Ogaden war the daily DC3 Air Somali *qat* flight to Mogadishu was always on time, and shooting at it from either side was a strict no-no. The brightly coloured, crumpled *qat* wrappings stick to every bush, so the people there call them "African roses".

Billy thought the scene at the hospital was the ultimate nightmare. He could not imagine what it must be like to live in a place where if people had any kind of accident this was where they would end up — if they could afford it. But he was determined to get through it, to be a man, gird his loins and will himself to watch with respect the atrocious tasks the hospital workers attend to on a day-to-day basis.

"It's fucking awful," he said to me, "but it's not a freak show."

"How on earth are you dealing with it?" I asked.

"Och, I just shut myself off. I go to this other place. I can do that. I can watch the most awful stuff without even being there."

I was worried about him. It is traumatising to witness pain and suffering on such a scale, and it seemed to me that Billy was dissociating, or stepping outside his body, in order to deal with it, an unhealthy return to his earlier coping method. There was an overwhelming sense of helplessness about the lives of many he met. One of the people whose progress the crew followed

256

was a three-year-old boy who'd been fighting for his life in the hospital. When he got home he was drinking the same water that had made him ill.

"But when I think of what he's faced compared to me," said Billy, "he's become a giant in my eyes. Such a brave little guy. By the time he's five, a quarter of his friends will be dead. My life is so easy."

On the second day, Billy was introduced to the "Lost Boys" as he named them, a bunch of homeless children who sleep in the street outside the police station. Their mothers had died and their fathers had flung them out on the street, either because they'd remarried or couldn't afford to keep them. They had all been attacked in a myriad of ways, bitten by animals, beaten up or sexually abused. A local policeman now kept an eye on them and tried to prevent them becoming junkies.

"They're a great bunch of kids," said Billy. "Full of life. Desperate to get out and do good for themselves. You got the sense they were quite enjoying being renegades, living free."

"You seem almost envious," I teased. Here was another echo to Billy's own past.

"Well, I felt we had a lot in common, me and the guys . . . and they were very relaxed with me," he said wisely. "I think people recognise these things in others. Synchronous attraction. You know you've survived something similar but you don't know quite what."

I understood it well. People who have survived similar abuses do seem to find each other. Billy and the film crew took all twenty of the Lost Boys to the township's one restaurant for breakfast. They were utterly thrilled and ordered the house speciality breakfast of liver and onions. These children normally went to the restaurant every day, but only to beg for scraps at the back door.

One of the Lost Boys steals extra food each day for his brother, a boy suffering from psychosis who is interred within the putrid enclosures of what is euphemistically called the hospital's psychiatric ward. In that place of utter horror, mentally ill people are chained to the walls and floors because there are no drugs to keep them stable. Tethered at a safe distance from each other, they are treated worse than animals in most zoos, their full range of motion being just three steps left and three steps right. As Billy stood confronted by this indescribable scene of people shuffling, rocking and shaking uncontrollably, one patient, bare-chested with a filthy lap cloth, stood completely still with hands crossed in front of him and head high, staring loftily.

"He's the President!" shouted his neighbour.

"Only sometimes," explained the warder to Billy. "Sometimes he's a general, and sometimes Muhammad."

"I must say, he looks very noble . . . if you ignore the chain on his leg."

The visual record of my husband in Africa made me very angry. For a start, the documentary crew had followed a young girl who had fallen down a hole. She eventually died because she could not afford the medical attention she needed.

258

"This is about poverty," said Billy earnestly to the camera's lens as he wandered zombie-like around the Hargeisa hospital. "These people need money very, very badly."

"Then tell their irresponsible government to crack down on the drug trade!" I shouted at the television.

I was so proud of Billy for his immense compassion. The experience challenged him in many ways, and he was having the kind of reaction all caring people from affluent communities have when they're faced with such misery: guilt about their relative societal and personal wealth. Yet he had given a tremendous amount, and had risked much just to be there in Hargeisa telling the story. And it wasn't as if he'd never known poverty. When he was crouched outside a rag hut saying, "The woman in there is giving birth on a dirt floor," I couldn't help thinking, "Well, that's not too far from how you came into the world, Billy."

After he'd been back home for a while, I finally had to break my silence.

"Billy," I ventured, "the whole thing's a shocking, tragic mess. I'm not even sure I agree with your being part of it. I mean, it's great to be charitable and give to Comic Relief so they can train health workers and so on, but someone should tell the truth about these corrupt governments and political debacles. If people weren't buying and selling qat on every street corner, then fathers wouldn't be spending all their money on drugs instead of food or medical care for their families. It's a vicious cycle and it should be busted. You saw the contraband planes yourself. Those Russian aircraft wouldn't be sitting at the foot of the runway if that government didn't allow it."

"Pamsy," he said, "I don't give a shit what their government does. I deal with the ordinary punter in a rotten position. We don't feed big fat soldiers and I don't believe in just giving handouts to people. We just make life better for the wee guys whose lives are a fucking disaster."

"And by the way," I challenged him, "what about that girl who died? Why didn't you pay for her to have the treatment she needed?"

"Pamsy," he said, "she was dead before I even landed in the country. The documentary makers just shot it backwards."

"Bloody hell," I said, absolutely furious. "People will think you could have saved her."

I knew that no matter how many people he could personally save there'd always be millions more who fell foul of a rotten system. I put my arm around him. "Must have been so hard."

"Yes," he said, a little shakily, "but I'm always deeply moved by their immense ability to stay alive, remain nice people and treat me well. That makes me feel hopeful."

I told him how enraged and helpless I had felt when I learned about the treatment of mental health patients.

"I got angry too when I was there," he confessed. "Whenever I raged about injustice, someone in dire straits would shrug his shoulders and say, 'It's the will of God.' That doesn't bode well. People take advantage of them for having that attitude. Of course they've been ripped off blind by politicians. What the African people need most of all is not clothing or shelter or medicines. They need someone to invent a special kind of arsehole-detector. They should stick it up at every parliament house like those screens you have to walk through at security. A sticky-finger detection device."

CHAPTER
TWELVE

A Genius
With Good Nipples

Those tie-dyed jeans he'd bought a few hours ago really did the job. Billy Connolly, sixty-year-old style-setter, voguish veteran and still-svelte swankster, caught sight of himself in a sports centre windowpane and, frankly, liked what he saw. It had not escaped his notice that the young saleswomen in the boutique that morning had swarmed around him, all compliments, courtesy and captivating cutie-pie. A frumpy woman about his age passed him at the doughnut shop, her head bowed.

He was feeling just a tad smug about the discrepancy in our culture, whereby women of a certain age become invisible to younger men, while aging men, especially those of power and means, seem all the more desirable in their later years. Just in time, he turned into the In and Out burger place. He had nearly forgotten his current mission, to pick up some fast food for Daisy who would shortly need a quick bite before the rigours of her Stage Combat class. As if by design, a gorgeous young Hispanic woman with three golden studs on each ear smiled adoringly at him as she took his order.

He supposed it was not out of the question that even some relatively young women could find themselves quite smitten with a suave, sexy and sophisticated man of the world like himself. He waited while she wedged the drinks in a cardboard tray and snapped the bag shut with a practised flourish.

"I believe that's everything," she smiled again, "and will you be wanting the senior discount?"

"I'm a sixty-year-old man and I can fucking dress myself," ranted Billy, the night he was honoured by the British Academy of Film and Television. I had made the mistake of trying to help him with the mock-military, three-piece tux he loves because it makes him look like the Mayor of Toy Town. A gold stripe ran the length of his black tuxedo trousers, while a gold-trimmed white waistcoat sat happily within a long black jacket with white-bordered lapels and a red-and-gold collar. A faux gold brocade medal dangled precariously from his left breast, as if to underscore the show of bravado that would be necessary from him tonight. Billy had been awfully nervous as the night approached.

"God, Pamsy," he whined, squeezing into black patent leather shoes with a cross-grain bow at each toe, "when people pay you tribute you feel duty-bound to be dead."

Peering uncomfortably in the bathroom magnifying mirror for a better chance at vanquishing his flourishing nose hairs, he eventually got nearer to the truth: "I feel like an impostor!" he confided.

But it is not only the survivors of childhood trauma who struggle with feelings of unworthiness; anyone who rises to public attention is liable to find it an intensely unsettling experience. As Montaigne said, fame and tranquillity can never be bedfellows. Our society's values give credence to the notion that success and acclaim lead to personal happiness. We thumb through the pages of *Hello!* magazine and imagine that all those happy pictures reflect a joy that is the result of achievement and recognition. In fact, for many people fame is a hollow victory, for it is profoundly disappointing to find they are essentially no happier than they were before.

Billy managed his rise to celebrity status better than many. Sometimes he just can't believe his luck, as was the case with his experience on *The Last Samurai*.

"There I was in Taranaki in New Zealand," he says, "a stunningly beautiful place with great fishing. I was wearing a Seventh Cavalry uniform riding a fabulous big horse, with a Winchester rifle strapped across my chest. On my right was Tom Cruise, and in the distance were some teepees, and as I rode thundering down the hill I remember thinking, 'You lucky boy!' But, at the same time, I also expected to look over my shoulder and see my old foreman saying, 'Billy, we're ready for you.'"

Driving to the BBC Television Studios in White City that night, he was powerfully silent. I was worried about him, and held his arm. It was stiff and trembling.

"I thought I fucking turned down this gig." He gritted his teeth. "No one ever listens to me . . ."

As soon as Billy saw Michael Parkinson, who hosted the show that night, he began to relax.

"Just you enjoy every single moment of it," smiled Michael kindly, sensing his discomfort. Since Billy's first appearance on his chat show in the 1970s, Michael has been his friend, mentor, erstwhile drinking buddy and accomplice in both humour and life. As they joked together in the dressing room I was relieved to observe that Billy was beginning to take the evening in his stride. He even helped sew me into my turquoise sequinned evening gown, a task with which he is quite familiar. Anyone who pops in to see us before a formal evening event is liable to be greeted by the sight of me bending over a piece of furniture while Billy sews my bra to the lowest part of my scooped-back dress. He's adorable when he tries to thread a needle, swearing savagely at it like a trucker with a broken power tool.

We gathered together in the studio. Among our many loyal, loving friends and show business acquaintances in the audience seats there was a thrilling sense of anticipation and camaraderie, but Billy again showed signs of apprehension, stroking his beard and shifting nervously as he waited backstage to be introduced. I was also on edge, for I had been asked to give a little speech at the beginning of the programme. It was a long time since I'd done anything like that. Billy and I huddled together in the wings while Michael gave an introductory welcome, then showed a clip of Billy and me performing together when we first met on *Not the Nine O'Clock News*. There we were, subtly flirting on camera, me as Janet Street-Porter in huge red spectacles and fake polystyrene teeth, and him in purple cowboy shirt. We were such an odd couple.

"Was it love at first sight?" asked Michael.

"I thought he was an intense beastie who had no business being outside the zoo," I replied.

It became quite clear throughout the evening that Billy's heroes didn't care about his preference for avoiding accolades. Jimmy Tarbuck began. "He's the best observation comic we've ever had," he said, "and he's got the balls of a lion. He goes into things . . . I've got no idea where he's going and neither does he until he gets started then he just has you on the floor . . . He's won, and quite deservedly."

Danny De Vito loomed on the screen seemingly unaware of the occasion. "They're giving him a Tribute? Happy Tribute, Billy!"

The clever Eddie Izzard turned up in a splendid evening kilt (a perfect choice for one who enjoys cross-dressing) and delivered a brilliant piece in a reverential tone:

I never wanted to be a stand up comedian, but I was told that I had to be one by God. He told me to look to the one from the north, who was from the west. I listened to his earlier recordings but they were hard to understand because they were in Elvish. And God said, "Look to the bit on incontinence knickers. It is good." And so I did. And it was good. "Just follow him, and he shall lead you from the land of 'my wife' jokes to the promised land of the comic philosophers. And he

shall be known as Moses to the Greeks, or Big Yin
to the Celts. And you shall know him as Billy."

Bob Geldof, who was given the task to talk about
Billy's musical abilities, roasted him about his early
folk-scene disasters.

"You can play a bit of banjo," he said, "but frankly,
who can't?"

One of the clips showed Billy singing a perfectly
awful folk song aboard a steamer on the Clyde. It was
shocking to see him looking so young, fresh-faced and
raw, with straggly brown hair and rotten teeth. Despite
his obvious lack of experience, he had a strangely
confident presence.

"I sound like a goose farting in the fog," Billy has
said, which isn't true, for his singing voice is really quite
beautiful. As I sat watching him on those early
folk-scene clips I was reminded that I often listened to
his music tapes in our early days together. To me Billy
was always such a romantic troubadour, standing on
stage in a moody spotlight, hugging his autoharp and
singing "Near You". I like to fantasise that he wrote that
song about me. I've never asked him because I don't
want to hear anything to the contrary.

> *I could sing you sad songs,*
> *Sing you songs to make you smile.*
> *I could sing you love songs*
> *But would that be worth my while*
> *When all I want to do*
> *Is be near you.*

267

"Billy Connolly is a genius," said Sarah Lancaster. "With good nipples."

It was a great surprise to see Eric Idle on video standing on a neighbouring island to the one on which we had all stayed just one month earlier. He and his wife Tania had sneaked off one day and filmed his absentee greeting. He was a wonderfully silly sight in his khaki shorts, knee socks and British Raj sun helmet:

"Hello, Billy! Sorry I can't be there tonight because . . . I'm . . . here." It was quite surreal. "So you're there and I'm here," he continued. "So sorry about the cock-up. And sorry this piece has turned out so lame."

Sir Michael Caine had to stay at home with flu, but he wrote Billy an appreciative note:

You are the funniest comedian I have ever met and the only one who wasn't depressed — a unique double whammy — but you have a third whammy, you are also a brilliant actor.

Chris Tarrant made a complaint. "Billy actually makes you ache."

I was mortified that they showed Billy naked and streaking around Piccadilly Circus in broad daylight for Comic Relief. I still cannot believe that he actually agreed to run that smiling, hands-high lap of honour in his birthday suit, even though it did raise a fortune for the charity. There was also a montage of Billy performing his bare-bum dance in several exotic world locations, the Arctic Circle and the Australian outback to name but two. In the former a digitally created snowflake danced strategically across his willy, and in the latter he finished his dance by mounting a huge Harley Davidson trike and thundering off into the sunset. Honestly! I hope he intended that to be satire, because otherwise he really took the "Men and their Macho Machines" theme just a little too far.

"He loves taking his haggis out," exclaimed Danny De Vito, who never spoke a truer word.

Billy had to resign himself to viewing all the video clips of his performances throughout his career so far: from his velvet flares and round face of his early folk days, his first gauche *Parkinson* interview, all giggles and sly looks, his sexy confidence on *Not the Nine O'Clock News*, and the brilliant stillness and power of *Mrs Brown*. It was all there, his engaging right-brain take on history in *World Tour of Scotland*, and his extraordinary body-humour pieces that produced screams every bit as loud as the first time.

"Pamsy . . ." Billy turned to me, quite unabashed to be caught giggling at his own comedy, "that stuff was awful funny. I think I'm beginning to understand what people see in me."

For Billy, the jewel was Dame Judi Dench. Reminiscing about her experience with him on *Mrs Brown*, she said he was one of the most professional actors she'd ever worked with. "He was inspirational and has become a fantastic friend. I absolutely adore him, and . . . one does love one."

Billy's heart leapt. I watched him accept all this glory relatively unflinchingly, and I sighed with great relief. Billy had made it through his year of living beigelessly.

Turning sixty had been accomplished, being honoured in this wonderful, heady way had been endured, and miraculously, the sky had not fallen in at any point.

What would his next decade bring? I wondered. For a start, there was bound to be more satisfaction in his ever-flourishing work.

"I just can't believe he's having a career growth spurt at his age!" I heard Steve his manager say before the show.

And then there would be ever more fun to be had, such as sailing his boat, teaching Walter to fish, and learning new tunes on his banjo. He stood on the stage, beaming in the spotlight and took his honour like a man.

"To be surrounded by people who like you is a wonderful thing and to be told one loves one by Judi Dench takes me straight to paradise. This is a very nice prize. I once won a pair of swimming trunks for winning the five-a-side football but they turned brown."

He proudly held the heavy platinum BAFTA mask, looked down at me for a moment and smiled mischievously. Then he turned to address the entire audience, who had risen to their feet.

"Thank you from the bottom of my heart," he said finally. "Now fuck off home and leave me alone."

The Seven Ages
Of Billy

All the world's a comedy club; and the men and women merely hopefuls in search of open-mike night. Most of them never top the bill, but all of them get seven cracks at it:

First the big wean, greetin' and girnin' in his mammy's bed, an evil-smelling thing of beauty, projecting awfulness from every orifice.

Then the spotty school boy, school bag and tide mark, stamps collected, plastic models glued, homework undone, being dragged into hell.

Then the lover, all Old Spice and hire purchase suits, clumsy footed on the dance floor, clumsy handed in the dark. He's desperate to be fancied, and hopes his voice breaks before his heart.

Then the soldier, swearing like a trooper, bright as a button, jumping from planes he's never had the money to travel in.

Next is the father, comfy chair and big daddy dinners, all advice and invented examples.

Then the sixth, big slippers and training bottoms, over-the-counter reading specs and over-the-bald-patch hairstyle. Knows the world well but can't remember where he left it. He turns to his banjo, but finds to his dismay that requests for "Somewhere Over the Rainbow" are actually directions to where he should practise.

There's a seventh but I'm not there yet, although I have noticed a creeping tendency to whistle and yodel during normal speech, and make involuntary noises when picking up heavy objects. And I'm looking forward to the day when a successful trip to the bathroom in the morning is every bit as good as sex.

There's an eighth age that Shakespeare forgot to mention. That's when they burn you at the crematorium and your pelvis and hips don't turn to powder because your joints don't break down. So they have to put you in a spin dryer, along with a metal ball about the size of a clenched fist. This big cricket ball pounds the big lumps enough to make them powder. After that you can go into a plastic box like a sweetie jar and your relatives will stand there um-ing and ah-ing about whether to get you transferred into the fancier one or not. Take my advice and make the most of the other ages while you're still too big for the sweetie jar.

When you're young's the time to get arseholed. Do not grow up! By all means grow old, but do not grow up. Growing old is great. It's just like getting drunk. Everyone around you gets better looking. You can stink up the place as much as you like, it doesn't matter;

you've lost your sense of smell by then, so who cares? Be as cranky as you like. Some time, when you're in a rotten mood, make a video of yourself so you can attack your family when you're dead. Don't trust anyone who says old people are nice. Some of them aren't. It's a sad fact of life that young arseholes become old arseholes. Don't worry if you start to die and haven't settled old scores. Grudges can always be carved on your gravestone, and granite lasts a long, long time. As you're about to slip into the dark void, and your eyelids close for the last time, you can afford to feel really smug, knowing you haven't returned your library books. If you really want to piss off your family, leave all your money to a home for bewildered banjo players.

If there's anyone you've forgotten to say goodbye to when you die, never mind. You can sit down with Bill Haley, sing "See You Later, Alligator" with him, and really mean it. And don't worry too much about the afterlife. You were made in God's image so you're probably going to get along just fine.